AF433076

Uncapped Feelings

T.Charles Rampedi

Published by T.Charles Rampedi, 2024.

While every precaution has been taken in the preparation of this book, the publisher assumes no responsibility for errors or omissions, or for damages resulting from the use of the information contained herein.

UNCAPPED FEELINGS

First edition. September 11, 2024.

Copyright © 2024 T.Charles Rampedi.

ISBN: 979-8227148650

Written by T.Charles Rampedi.

Also by T.Charles Rampedi

Notebook
Through My Pen
Uncapped Feelings

Table of Contents

I had a dream about you
Me and you.
We were seated on the couch dazzling each other with words that made you blush and smile like eternity came to see and told me welcome to heaven
The girl standing next to me
It was all just a blur
That's when I fell, and you fell over me
What did it mean?
Did it represent me falling in love with you, and you falling for me
On the ground I was able to see you perfectly
In my arms I was able to see the beauty that hid between your smile
As you were giggling the words you said, made me high even though I cannot recall them
You said them with a beautiful gaze while looking in my eyes
Free spirited self you were smiling
You were happy
And we turned to kiss
And I was enchanted by the lips of both I and you meeting
Like strawberries I was never denied their color
As I closed my eyes to get an alluring savor
After that majestic kiss
I turned to open my eyes, and you were gone
A river of lava was burning around I
I ran from the house you were in, to the other
As I arrived at the door it was locked
I knocked and knocked with my breath fading
I turned to open the door and landed in a room that seemed like mine
I looked at myself on the mirror trying to control my heavy breath, but I could not
I took off my hoodie and shirt

Sat down on the floor to let the coldness sink in my lungs to stop me from feeling the way I felt
But I couldn't
So, I shouted out the pain
Just to realize, it was just another dream
A dream about you.

Define love, the meaning of it, a lot of words have been used to describe the feelings that revolve around that word, but none seems to match that feeling. None seem to be perfectly describing it, like my uncapped feelings. It's strange how life changes from generation to generation. All worldly wonders turn to change, so do feelings, and even love is no longer the same as that of the past. People get lost in the errors of this world, one might say it has always been said, "seek wisdom from those that possess the hair that looks white or gray like the clouds up in the heavenly skies". In other words, with age comes wisdom, so seek it from those who possess it, for you to be wise. Well with this generation, wisdom is taken as something that involves control while it is to set a path, to guide, or heed. Those who seek it tend to get lost, as it doesn't go with the so-called "today-style". It's either you become an outcast with the wisdom passed down to you or one of the crew without it, and loneliness turns to lurk on the streets searching for those lone wolf outcasts to do damage.

Seated with my mother, talking about this new generation which I'm in. Talking about the whole gender issues of this world, stating that feelings don't turn out to have anything to do with your gender, feelings are all about expression, the way we used to know and grew up knowing. Expressing your emotions about how you feel towards a certain subject or something. With gender, a gay was a man who had the sexual reproductive organ of a female, and a lesbian was a woman who had the sexual reproductive organ of a male, who were called "tona kasadi" in my home language.

These days all kids turn to say they are gays and lesbians, and now the titles of gender have even increased a lot because they turn to say they feel like they were supposed to be something else. Like the man who said he feels like he was supposed to be a dog, now he lives like one, or that other one who said he feels like he was supposed to be a baby, ironic.

Sleeping with someone and not feeling a certain way doesn't mean you must be attracted to the opposite gender; it just means that your spirit doesn't quite sit well with that person. It's like the saying, intercourses before marriage aren't right as quoted. Having it with a random person isn't going to sit well with your spirit, and remember, some of us, our spirits are hard to understand. That's why we mostly get lost and find whatever reason it is suitable to put on and say yes this is the reason, but what do I know, I am just old. Let this gray hair be my witness, I know nothing but the old, and this is the new, but the new needs to be made while looking at the old sometimes.

For me, if I turn to look at it with a certain eye, if it were me, and I was searching for something and the path I took isn't showing any progress that I'm going to find it, an alternative way has to be found which is going to lead me to having what I want, need sweets, and have no money, ask they say pay, but you have no money, you beg, you cry, and get angry, you take it, "steal it", to be more accurate, we all did it when we were young, even if it's not based on stealing we all once took the easy way out. What's to change about love, politics, finding a job, etc.? We still do it.

Choose the easiest path to find what we seek but hard to approach it. It's hard to witness failure, and multiple times rips you apart to collapse, it's hard. Even with love, when it's hard to find love, or you do, but keep on falling in love with the wrong person over and over again and getting hurt, but you seek it with a lot of affection with all your heart, you turn to form an alternative, adapt to the pain, or change what you seek by just a little factor.

Maybe it was I who took the alternative of finding what I sought for, or the signs on the road weren't interpreted in a way I could sign them. Was it I or her that took the alternative?

Chapter One

Love, a picture that was painted in my brain, a canvas so beautiful the word itself underrated it. In my brain it was painted but the thought of it never came. It all started with the search for friendship, someone to play with at a young age. When I was young, I grew up having a friend from kindergarten, he was my best friend, and I believed that it was a friendship which was going to last till eternity. We ended up going to the same primary school together, but after attending there for two years, his family had to move, which left me lonely as I didn't have any other friend besides him. So, I grew up transitioning from a friend to a friend which was what I got used too, even though it stopped during the moment when high school started introducing itself to me. Some may say that transitioning is called loneliness as you would never see me spending time together with a specific person everyday but always moving around groups of my peers like a puppy looking for its owner in a crowded area.

After losing him I was found alone by another in second grade, and we became knotted like brothers from different mothers, a childhood worth deserving of the name, and countless times I've spent with him, playing together, exploring the mountain, little forest, and the fields around our place. But in life all things must end, even with that magnificent friendship.

I found refuge under the friendship of my neighbor Jack, who I grew up with, but was never allowed to play with him, due to his family not liking mine. Every time I would go to play at his house, they would always call him inside to watch television, and I'd watch it from the window or at the door, going to play on the streets with other kids or just us two, he was told not to go anywhere. A friendship that never started and never finished, like dust carried by the wind. Television became my friend, watching cartoons and movies, music became my solace, and writing (poetry, music, short stories and drawing as hobbies) became my voice. A childhood filled with only that, and my young brother also removing the boredom by playing games together, no other friends, even he had friends and wasn't always around to hang out much. A realization came upon me before departing to high school that the world has changed, and I too require a friend, a brother from another mother or sister. The term loneliness was not known to I, as I described it as "original".

With new beginnings ahead, new friendships to be made in high school, all hopes were raised to a level no limit has ever risen. A great adventure was laid in front of me, an adventure that soon turned to be clouded by darkness. When I arrived in high school students already had friends, even freshmen already had friends on the first day. Which demolished my plan to find a friend. That was when I decided to shrug myself and let the friend that I was searching for find me, but he never did. I told myself that if a friend doesn't want to be found, a girlfriend was suited for me, for with a girlfriend you can share more than what the heart has to say, more of how your soul speaks, and the quest to find her began. Definition of a girlfriend, I never knew, do you know in order to find a girlfriend you must have feelings, even though you write for expression, the expression stated on the papers needs to be heard by that person you're looking for, searching for a girlfriend, is searching for love. I never knew love, I had feelings, but never thought of love as something that I would desire. The picture of a girlfriend was painted differently in my mind compared to the one of love, and so, the year passed with me spending all my time with my hobbies, drawing, writing poetry, music, and short stories by myself. It was a good year, not knowing the amount of pain to arise the coming year.

When the new year approached, during the school days, I was seen writing something in my book vibing with it by shaking my head. One of the students in my class got curious and during lunchtime, when I was out eating my lunch, he went to my bag which I left in class and took the book I was writing in. When I came back, I found him at the back of the class laughing with his friends huddled up, keened to something that was placed on the table. I continued with my business by minding my own, placed my lunch box in my bag, and the laughter became more annoying, jokes being thrown, some even acting upon what was written, in my presence. The laughter that you could see that it's seeking your attention. I zipped my bag and blocked out their laugh, shifting my mind to think about something else, getting the idea that they were laughing at me. I decided to leave and as I was about to step out of the door, one of them called me up, not by name, as my name was not known.

"Dude is your brain functioning," he yelled directing it to me.

Puzzled, I turned and looked at the corner of the class. One of the guys raised my book, and a huge pain gushed to my gut, it felt like I was being punched in the stomach. I turned and headed their direction, with my chin up, while they were laughing insanely trying to get me angry, mocking me, quoting words from the poems I've written and songs, as I arrived to the one who was holding it, I snatched it from his hand, and went to my bag. They followed me pushing me around, laughing loudly in my ear, I grabbed my bag, checked if everything was in there, placed my book in and left the class with it to buy snacks. The choice that I made was to keep it low, and now that choice was at risk, that day I barely survived.

To my thought it was the worst day ever, not knowing it was just a small fire, a little spark that almost caused a blazing fire, for the blaze was still yet to come. I never thought the year might get any worse, but it did. It's known that high school is a place to leave a mark, a good mark for being the top achieving student, best at sports, best bullied students, etc. A mark which you'll be remembered by your classmates and teachers. For me, I was better alone and minding my own business and trying to leave high school and not be remembered at all or as the quiet guy, but that never happened. After that incident with the guys another one followed, and this time with a girl, a humiliation that ripped my reputation into pieces. I never had a reputation in school,

I was never known, but after that fight I was known, destroying the nothing I had, into a word that describes what comes after nothing.

The girl I had a fight with accused me of stealing a mechanical pencil, which was similar to hers, and I used mine to draw only. After losing hers, she saw mine and the feud started there, an argument that heated up and started attracting every single student in class and the worst part was that the teacher wasn't in that day, which meant it was a free period. Lasting up until after school. A guy can't hit a girl that is known, or in my favor that was what I promised my mother to never do as I used too when I was young, and through the name-calling, with teenagers laughing stupidly so, dragging my face to make a face-off with her, and the amount of words I tried speaking, silenced by the heart I had. I was trying to calm my heart, my rage, and the tears that I wanted to let out. It felt like I was thrown into a cage of wild animals screaming and banging the cage. All the students were all over us, as she said whatever words she wanted to say to win the battle, forced to listen to everything.

As the bell rang, to signal that it was time to go home, my heart was heavy with anger, my brain thinking about the outcomes of what just happened, if it really did happen, if it were just a dream, maybe I'll wake up, but it wasn't. While I was waiting for my transport to take me home, I saw a lot of students point at me, laughing, and I saw her walking with a group of students smiling, and given the glory. I broke. One tear dropped from my eye, I quickly tried to remove it and get a hold of myself, but my heart was already relieving itself, my lungs were already removing the anger I had on my chest that suffocated my heart, a river was already floating down my cheeks, and I couldn't stop anything, I just broke. Believe it reader, my emotions were seen by everyone passing, a guy was crying, I was crying. Shattering everything. Raising my fists would've ended that war but I couldn't, only tears were left to console me as my transport mates watched and tried to sooth. My unknown name became a joke.

That little plan that I had about there being a friend looking for me, searching for a girlfriend, crumbled to ashes. I was the main topic during that week, which made me lock myself up and become lonely. The week passed to months, from months to a year, and I found myself in the 10th grade sitting alone with no friends but my mind occupying me with jokes and reminding me of funny clips I saw in movies to make me happy and smile, and that reader is what we classify as weird, as I was found laughing out loud with tears rolling down my face not knowing what I was laughing at. I was lonely and had no friends, all my hobbies became my friends. During free periods when students were talking with their friends, playing games, I was cooped up by myself, drawing, I ate alone, I did most things alone, until I realized that I was lonely when I heard one of my classmates telling his friend who didn't want to go buy snacks with them that he wants to be alone and lonely, singing the song called Lonely by Akon, teasing him until he stood up and went with them. I should try and find friends, someone to talk to, because I wasn't mute, I could talk, but I had no one to talk to about the adventures my brain takes me too. An idea came, since I was known at school for being the loser who got bullied by a short girl, I decided to go on the internet to look for a friend. But the internet wasn't that friendly at all.

I created a Facebook account in hopes of finding new friends, people to talk to, but it was all just an imagination and what it was created for is not what it resembled. People only cared about the amount of likes you had on your posts, the comments, how pretty you are, beauty became the key to opening a conversation, likes became the description of the type of person you are. My interest in it became less and I started visiting the website sometimes to check on what people are doing and the latest trends rather than talking to anyone, and sometimes became partially. I spent most of my time playing games on my phone, rather than going on the website, until I lost interest in it.

Until I got a friend request from her, Pearl Alexandra "Alex" Chen.

Chapter Two

Like a rose, her beauty was flawless, with her smile stylish like the curves of a rose peddle, her eyes like the aroma it gives, always calling you for more, her lips infused with its color but fluffy like the clouds up in the heavenly skies. A perfect creation. Pearl was a one-of-a-kind beauty that outshines all the beauty present. Reader she was beautiful.

But beauty in my eyes had to be earned, it's not always that I get to use this word on everyone, but she was beautiful.

I took notice of the notification coming from the website about a friend request and I accepted it, with the expectation of getting a message which says, "please like my photo", as usual. Expectation. Expectations sometimes do turn to kill, worst when they are made by the heart. A heart can be broken by just one little thing that doesn't go the way you expected it to go.

A message was received saying "Hi" immediately after accepting that friend request. I replied the same way and left the website to play a game. Another notification from the website rang;

"How are you?", it said.

"I'm fine and you," I replied.

"Fine, I'm Pearl Alexandra Chen".

Confusion drew near, no one in this modern-day world greeted nor introduced themselves in this manner, especially girls, what you might get might be a silly nickname or a fake name but not a full name. Why would she even text me and introduce herself? "Maybe she will ask after the introduction for the likes and comments" was my thought.

"Uhm, okay, still living in the olden days I see, you know you could have just said your name is Pearl, or Alexandra or Alex in short, I would've caught that," I replied.

"Like for instance, I'm Dimpho, see".

"Well, Dimpho, I decided to give you a choice to pick a name you'd call me with, and it seems like you chose Alex since you shortened Alexandra like everyone else".

I was given an option to choose a name to call her, at that moment I was utterly confused, for why would I choose a name to call her by, she was a stranger. It seemed like I was minutes away from establishing a friendship that I longed for, but doubt was still present in my gut. A conversation that started like that was weird and my first time experiencing it, was she looking for a friend or something, for me it was too good to be true and weird. I told myself that she was just bluffing, give it time, and it will all disappear, let the time only tell.

"What if I want to call you Pearl and choose to be different from the others".

"Whatever you choose, will be fine for me Mr. Artist".

"I'm not an artist," I said confused, wondering where she got that type of information.

"Well, your timeline says otherwise," she said.

Everything started aligning, in my account, I posted music recommendation, some of the songs that I used to make, lyrics, poems, quotes and videos. I forgot about those, meaning that before talking to me, she must have done her homework. So, I quickly went to her page, to see if I couldn't find any information about her, strangely, I found nothing about her. No pictures, no posts, nothing, it was a ghost town. I told her that I wasn't an artist, I just do those things because I get bored, and get lonely sometimes, rather, most of the time.

She responded by saying, "So you basically write based on how you feel about yourself, I like that".

"Yeah, but why is your bio empty, as well as your timeline?", was my response, I had to know because she knew something about me, out of curiosity, it was necessary, it was a demand to know.

"Well, there's nothing much interesting about me, that's why everything is blank, because I am blank".

"I highly doubt it," I said, trying to at least get her to say something about herself, "I'll be the judge of that".

"I'm serious though".

"Really?".

"Okay, since you don't believe me, ask me anything, and then you'll see what I mean when I say I'm living a boring life", finally giving me the go ahead to ask questions, and of course I did not hesitate, I just short the first question.

"Alright, the first question is where are you from?"

She took a little time to respond to the message and replied, "I'm from Elinor".

Well, I got excited, because I have spent most of my time there, since I was enrolled in Crestwood Academy. I felt like it was finally happening, as if the tale was unrevealing itself, but one thing was certain, if she was from around Elinor, it was possible that she might know me from the incident with the girl. Or might have heard stories or rumors, but I pushed that away, for the first time in my life, someone was talking to me, not because she wants help, or needs something. But for the fact that it was just the start of a conversation, and all my intentions disappeared, I was no longer curious, my heart was open. I was finally about to make a new friend, the name Elinor, faded all my loneliness, and limited the doubts that I had about her.

"No way, I spend most of my time in Elinor, I'm enrolled in Crestwood" I said.

"Really." she said.

"Yeah, mind sending me your picture maybe I might bump into you sometimes, or already did, who knows".

"Alright".

I received two pictures from her, one half face, she was smiling, her cheeks perfectly aligned with her nasolabial folds, her pink lips perfectly bringing out her brown glazed eyes like an annular eclipse, with her hair tied long behind, and the other one she was dressed in a white dress, and with short hair, she was perfect. Unfortunately, I didn't recognize her, I've never seen her before.

"Sorry but I don't recognize you, but I have to say that you look beautiful though," I said admitting it.

"Maybe that's because I'm enrolled in Rutherford, and thank you," she replied with blushing emojis.

I saw the message, but decided not to open it and respond, leaving the site to focus on my game. It wasn't a dreadful thing to leave Pearl without responding to her message, it was a normal routine for me, spending 30 minutes on the website watching videos, what people are doing, I used it to keep up to date with the latest trends. I regarded it as the usual, even though I was excited a few moments ago about meeting her, nothing changed about the way I felt about people that I meet online, I still believed that it was always a 2-minute thing, and 30 minutes was even a lot, because I was used to just scrolling and scrolling.

As days went by, I found myself frequently visiting her pictures, staring at them, I was smitten. It seemed like I was starting to develop feelings for this total stranger, a stranger who I haven't talked to for the past four days. It might have been a possibility that Pearl was just a thing of the moment, like a visitor who came to check if I was still breathing or not. So, I did what I thought was best for me, I deleted the photos and went on my way to living my normal day-to-day lifestyle of watching movies, doing homework, doing music, and drafting poems. I ignored and forgot about her.

Two more days passed, with a mind that seemed confused. A mind that was dreaming about the impossible, feeding the heart beliefs and lies about there being true love in between the messages that I used to receive days ago. Illusions kept approaching from different sides, blocking my focus, a heart pounding louder than what I can hear, every time I daydreamed, movies that included romance would be shifted to the perspective where it was experienced by me and her. That night, sleep became my brains enemy, as I thought about her, contemplating with my thoughts, imagining scenes seen from movies infused with I and her. I couldn't take it anymore, so I did what my brain thought best to do in order to get some sleep. I went to the bin, and found the two photos, restored them back to my gallery, and began looking at them as if I was enchanted, under a love spell. Thoughts went away when I stared at the photos, and I could hear myself breathing and my heart beating for the first time, peace. Was I in peace? For all the voices in my head were silent, the voices that I grew up with, the friends I had in my head, voices I counted on and listened to when they were indulging me with tales never told, adventure never seen, now silent like the graveyard.

When midnight struck, I turned to ask myself what was happening, why am I feeling this way? I decided to take my headphones and listen to sad music, since sad music defines me, tells stories about me, find voices that speak to my feelings, prepares me for disappointment, so I don't get hurt when it comes. But this time it was different. Every sad song I listened to started sounding like a love song, which was about being sad but finding her as my silver lining. Minutes into the playlist, I decided to go on the site to respond to her message. I avoided talking to her for almost a week, I was certain that her response wasn't going to avail itself on my notification box, why should she respond for I ignored her, but I took the chance to just do it, just to shut down the loud beating lub dub drums of my heart I had at the moment. It was weird for me, because those feelings I felt, I've never felt them before, the meaning of them was a mystery to me.

"Yeah, maybe that's why," I replied.

It was a good move to text her in the middle of the night, as expectations were less, and I believed that Pearl wasn't going to respond. It was 00:37 a.m. as usual most people are asleep at that time, but I never knew that she also was like I. She immediately replied to my message,

"Your back, I thought you left me," she said.

I was shocked that she replied, and immediately after sending her the text, she was awake.

"Sorry, I was working on something," I lied, my insecurities weren't about to be shared with her, a stranger.

"And why are you awake at this hour, I'm the only one who stays up till this time".

"Well, I was just thinking about something, and no, you're not the only one", I was intrigued at this stage.

"Let me guess, you're also listening to music as well," she said.

"Are you stalking me?".

"Haha, no, it's just a hunch, I turn to do that when I can't sleep".

"Alright. So, what have you been up to?".

"Wondering where you wandered off to".

"Like I said, thinking, but I'm here," I said, forgetting the fact that I told her that I was working on something.

"Okay, well It's late now for us to talk, so I think we should go to sleep, we've got school today, and then, you can call me after school to let me know what you were thinking of for the past six days, is that cool?", she said, was it a smooth talk? It's normally boys who do the smooth talk reader, but in this case was it a smooth talk?

"Okay, I'll call you then," I told her excitedly.

"Okay," she said, sent me her number and said, "Good night".

"Night".

The first good night text I've ever got from a girl.

Chapter Three

If you desire something with all your heart, but it seems impossible for you to get it, an alternative must be created. I was searching for a friend, but with just a small scent of words, butterflies in my stomach were born. Was it an alternative that I took or was it her alternative to smooth talk me the way she was. The game was supposed to be brought by me, as a guy, but this time a girl made the moves, which was weird, and no game was ever going to be forged by my name as my intentions weren't aimed to the point where it was all heading to.

I tried to close my eyes to finish the night with a little bit of rest, but the joy I felt deep down wouldn't allow it. So, I stayed up through the night staring at the ceiling and playing thoughts about me and her being together. The clock tick to clock clockwise without a thought of anticlockwise, I was happy. The sun turned to notice my smile and rose quickly in disbelief to see my smile for the first time, with sweet melodies of birds singing in the early morning breeze that sent chills up my spine, but still refreshing, like the thoughts a newborn baby has. I woke up and prepared to go to school, but before hopping out of bed, I turned to take a last-minute glimpse of the night if I was in a dream or reality. I visited the conversations I had with her, to a touching amusing enchantment, it was real.

I went to school with a bright smile, which this time was a real smile, not a fake pretense. During one of the free periods, when some students were busy writing homework requested for the class on Monday, some talking about what they were going to do that weekend, I saw myself writing a note to myself, a poem to state my feelings aloud. In my mind, the meaning of writing was to calm myself down and deescalate the feelings a little bit, but my mind was somewhere else during that time, not on Pearl. One of the greatest things about writing a note is that you express your feelings and place your feelings and thoughts on a piece of paper, without reading it back. I wrote it, but never read what I wrote at that time.

After arriving home after school, before doing my homework, I decided to read what I wrote during class. An unexpected and yet expected turn was viewed and felt by my soul. What I had written wasn't just a note, but a love note expressing my feelings towards Pearl, I was falling head over heels for her, the love note written read;

Darkness is what I fear a lot

Most of the time I seem to be spending it locked up within it

I'm still in the dark but lately, it doesn't quite seem that scary anymore

A thousand voices I heard while cooped up in the middle of nothing turned to be synchronized to a single beating sound of harmony

A beating of lub dub

The chills I felt have gone with the freezing moist of rain

I can feel the warmth right in between the chest that was suffocating, barely breathing

Don't get me wrong, I'm still in the dark

But this darkness feels different from the one I know

My face has been trying to pull up strings to make me smile like my lips are a puppet

The air I taste is mesmerizing, my lungs are delighted and thankful

I sometimes feel like I recognize this place I'm in even though its pitch black from front to back

It's weird how the lub dub drums seem to be changing pace every time I recognize a certain change in my dark place

I don't know what it is

But surely this little fix may be tinkered with for the first time in a lifetime

Or tinkered to be sent deeper into the clutches of the pitiful dark deep void.

I realized that what I've written seems to be a love note expressing how I was before meeting her, the stage where I am since she introduced herself to me. But I couldn't believe it as I wasn't thinking of her during the time when I was writing this. So, I quickly freshened up and started doing my homework, but I was destructed by the thought that I had fallen for her, in just mere seconds. In my eyes, a person can't gain feelings or fall for someone in just a moment, without even meeting the person in real life to see if she exists or not, without even going out on a date, without knowing the person in life fully, to just fall over a two-minute conversation. I closed my books and told myself that I'm going to write a love note to her, and if the poem is good, then it settled it, I had fallen for her, but if it were just a poem just like any other it would mean I was just going crazy.

I took out my Notebook, took a pen, took my phone, inserted headphones, and started listening to sad songs, and began writing.

Am I falling for you? I think I am

Or I have already fallen for you

I know it's stupid and impossible to fall for someone in just mere seconds, and I know it is possible

But only on love at first sight even though my heart has told me that just happens in the movies only

In this case, it is not love at first sight but love at first text, maybe

But it seems I lost sight and the sight I see is only a scene of you

My mind has been under maintenance since moments after chatting with you, building up dreams that reality might deny

While my heart is pounding hard with a wrecking ball breaking the broken dreams I had about love and life

Replacing them with new ones made in your image

I think I'm going crazy cause I can't seem to stop thinking about you

Now I'm just wondering if you ever smiled at our conversations as I blush the bubbles when they are written "typing..."

Does your heartbeat twice to create suspense when thinking of something to say

Or maybe it is all just in my head, my head is crazy, and do have a big one

That's why it made a construction site in my thoughts just to think of you

It's weird how I never loved and know nothing about love but the love I got is an itch in my hand wanting to grab my phone and text you, call you, and tell you that I love you

Well, it is too soon for that

But in my head, I've already said it

And in my heart, we're living together a happy life

I finally can define happiness and that's with you.

I took the Notebook, stood up, turned off the music, and began reading it repeatedly. It started making sense, it was true, I was catching feelings that fast. I expressed my feelings perfectly, but I didn't like the fact that I was falling in love with someone that fast. So I took upon the decision to never express these feelings, rather wait until I was fully sure that I know Pearls flaws and perfections, wait and give it time, maybe it's just a thing of the moment, and if my heart still beats for her I will do it, once I know her fully, and if knowing her would lead me to discover shady things about her, I would be protected. I then read the note again, and in doing so, one line reminded me that she asked me to call her after school. I took the book and placed it on my study desk, took my phone and dialed her number, it rang the first time, and on the second ring, she picked up.

"You called," she said with a little bit of a silent hidden chuckle.

Chapter Four

Reader, it's strange if you think about it, the way the mind works when the levels of dopamine, serotonin and oxytocin have reached their full capacity, with the desire to exceed it. The way they influence the brain into thinking the impossible, why not regard it as peer pressure as the hormones influence one another, influencing the brain, from the brain to the heart, from the heart to making the soul believe that it has found its soulmate. If I were to ask if those hormones weren't available, were we going to fall in love the same way we do or would the sophisticated metaphors that the brain makes when the heart starts becoming fluffy and the butterflies in the stomach moves to its direction, the lungs trying to take in the breeze but feels so delightful making it hard to breath as it tickles the trachea, weren't available. Will falling in love become so dull and ending love become magnificent, as falling in love is so beautiful and mesmerizing at the start but losing it is hard. I wonder how aquatic creatures fall in love because they always seem to be at peace, like listening to her voice.

Her voice sounded like water splashing through the rocks and rubbles, providing that harmonic sound infused with the breeze that moved across the sound of the leaves on the trees and grass whistling tunes only fairies produced. Her voice sounded peaceful like I was lost in the creek that looks better than any imagination can draw. Not only that, but her giggle was like the flowers aligning next to the floating stream attracting butterflies to come and take a glimpse of a scenic beauty only stars saw and perfected for only eyes of the worthy to see. It sounded majestic, no lie can be told by those lips, for the smile that was brought on my face was speaking tales of love, with a huge adrenaline gut punch felt, telling me to lay on the bed and close my eyes to get lost in it.

In which I did reader, laid on my bed to get lost in her voice.

"As instructed, I did".

"Took you long enough," she said giggling.

"You've got issues, I still called though", I responded while laughing.

"Yeah, I get it, you were still trying to figure out what to tell me, or maybe you were nervous, afraid to talk to me," she said teasing me.

"Nah, I had to finish my homework first, so I can watch movies during the weekend," I said trying to calm myself, as my heart was pounding fast, and I couldn't catch my breath, trying to balance it accordingly. I never finished my homework; I was busy trying to figure out if I was falling for her or what.

"Oh, what type of movies do you like watching," she said.

"Romance, animation, comedy and horror".

"Oh, I love horror movies, most especially when Halloween approaches, a lot of horror movies are played during October, it's so awesome, it's weird how they make them, the blood splash, the pop-up scare, and did you see the comedy ones of scary movie franchise", she giggled, "that guy with the scream mask saying waaaaasup! Waaaaasup! then they would be like hey pick up the phone, waaaaasup! Waaaaaasup! Waaaaaasup! not knowing that they are going to die", she started laughing, "and that girl who the guy chopped her head and was still talking, like I'm not scared at you, oh boo hoo, you're supposed to be scary, ohh no, and got so annoyed and threw the head in the trash, and she kept talking, or Freddy Krueger vs Jason, that one is the best, including Annabelle" she said adding a giggle.

Reader, Pearl was talkative, and I loved it, I stood quite listening to her as she was talking about the Scary Movie franchise and other movies. After hearing her giggle, I couldn't help but burst with laughter, with my cheeks contracting, becoming round, and hurting. She heard me laughing, and she giggled a little adding;

"Yeah, I know, I talk a lot", she said with a sense of embarrassment.

"I can see that, I don't talk much, but it's amazing to listen to you... hear you talk a lot," I chuckled.

"Well unfortunately I might cause you to talk too much too, and besides you can't just listen to me talk, it's not fair, I also want to listen to your voice".

"Okay, I guess I'll try to talk (If you give me the chance)", I chuckled.

After teasing her, she was quiet for a moment.

"So, what have you been thinking about for the past six days for you to not text me back," she said with her smooth angelic voice, saying it slowly, changing the topic.

"Some stuff, you know," I said dodging the question.

"I guess, I think I'm like you, but I turn to do a lot of stuff, and I talk to myself a lot, that's why I'm a little bit weird", she laughed.

"Really... a little bit?".

"Okay, a lot then! I mean, it's not my fault that I don't have people to talk to".

"Okay, but... I still want to know a little something about you".

"Like what?".

"Well, anything about you... that's about you".

"You want to know more about me, huh? Well... let me tell you, I'm a total psycho..." she laughed," just kidding! Okay, okay, I'll behave. So, I'm a total horror movie buff, like I mentioned earlier. I love getting scared out of my wits! There's something about the thrill and adrenaline rush that just gets me going. My sister even thinks I'm crazy, but hey, being a little weird is what makes life interesting, right? When I'm not watching horror movies or talking to myself (just kidding, that's all the time), I love to read, listen to music, and try new foods. I'm a total foodie at heart, even though I can't cook" she laughed.

"But enough about me, let's talk about you! What's your excuse for being so charming and handsome? (just kidding, sort of)", she giggled. "So, tell me, tell me, what's something that you're passionate about? Or something that makes you go all nerdy and excited? And don't even try to give me short answers, I want all the juicy details; I'm settled in with my popcorn and movie, ready to listen to everything about you. Oh, and by the way, I just saw the most iconic scene in The Shining... you know, the "Here's Johnny!" moment, like literally shivers, still gives me the chills every time. But anyway, back to you, what's your secret obsession? Don't worry, I won't judge (much)".

"But you already know what I'm passionate about, you saw my timeline and bio on my Facebook account".

"Nooo! You think you're sneaky, don't you? Trying to turn the tables on me! Oh, yes! I did snoop around your Facebook profile (and don't pretend like you didn't do the same to me, even though mine is empty)", she chuckled. "And yes, I saw your interests and bio. But that's just scratching the surface, I want to know what makes you tick, what gets you excited, and what you're passionate about in your own words. Facebook profiles can be so... superficial, don't you think? That's why my account is empty, besides, I've been thinking... maybe there's something you're passionate about that you haven't shared on social media. Something you only reveal to people you really trust... like me, perhaps?", she added with a sense of shyness.

"Well, I think the reason why your account doesn't say much about you, it's because you have too much to say, you might end up causing a malfunction on the website with what you want to share," I said laughing.

"Hey!", she shouted softly, "that's not nice, don't say that", she giggled, and a little silence was introduced.

"Why so quiet?" I burst with laughter.

"Your and idiot you know that...I don't want to talk to you anymore".

I chuckled, "Okay, I'm sorry, I was kidding".

"Big head," she said quietly.

"Aah, see".

"No! You started it!" she said laughing.

We spent the whole afternoon playing a game of one question one answer to get to know each other better, teasing and mocking each other, even though playing it with her made it one question one story telling, it was fun, I seemed to have achieved what I desired, a friend to talk to, worst part, my own radio, and reader, it's a complement.

We got well acquainted, and in the middle of the conversation my sister came to my room to call me, because it was dinner time. I delayed for a couple of seconds, the seconds turned to minutes, and the minutes turned to an hour, and the conversation had to be cut off. I might have been in love, but I also loved food, especially when the food is still hot fresh from the pots not the microwave. But mine were now cold, and so we had to say our goodbyes.

Chapter Five

Our goodbyes turned into, "are you sleeping" conversations. After eating, I washed the dish, completed my homework, and went to watch a movie with my family. When the 11 o'clock clock, clocked, I went to my room to try and get some rest, and as I laid on my bed, before sleeping I took my phone and connected the headphones to listen to music and obviously, the normal routine of watching the two photos she once forwarded to me, and started daydreaming. I took my phone and placed it next to me and closed my eyes, smiling and placed my hands on my chest to start thinking about her. I started laughing to myself, giggling while thinking about the conversation we had had earlier that afternoon. Likewise, I couldn't help but to just let the laughter out, making me lose control, an unbelievable expectation that occurred. I twisted and turned, laid with my belly on the bed with my arms under the pillow so when I laughed and giggled with excitement, the pillow might catch the sound and keep it to itself too, for it's been so long for it to taste joy as well.

While still in my thoughts, a ringing sound interrupted my thoughts and the music, I took my phone with intentions to put it on silent, so I can listen and think about her properly, just to find a notification from her, it read;

"Are you sleeping?".

Obviously, I wasn't, I was still trying to let everything sink in, I was still replaying that reality which felt like a dream. I was still dreaming about the possibilities of her, the girl who just texted seconds ago.

"Not really", was my response.

"What are you doing?", she asked.

"I'm listening to music and thinking about some stuff".

"Your always thinking, what are you thinking about, indulge me with your thoughts".

Unfortunately, if she knew that my thoughts were occupied with the thought of her, indulging the heart with a conversation far from reality made in her beauty. That my heart and brain were acting like best friends bragging about the type of dreams they dreamed about her, how was she going to feel. Unfortunately, I couldn't say.

"The conversation we had earlier on," I replied.

"Oh, so you were thinking about me," she said sending a laughing emoji.

"I said conversation, not you".

"Relax, I'm just teasing".

"Anyway, why are you up, detective?"

"I can't sleep, so I'm doing what you're doing".

With that being said, it seemed as if our thoughts were occupying themselves with depictions of each other.

"What time are you going to sleep?" she asked.

"I don't know".

"Want to continue the conversation from earlier".

"Okay".

And so the conversation continued, we talked about different horror movies, novels we both read, finding out what we had in common, even diving into fashion, arguing about who is tall in between me and her, she was, but I couldn't just let her win on that, I'm a guy, so I am taller than her, since I liked her, I had to be, it was necessary, playing all possible scenarios of life, it felt like we covered almost all the topics any person might have ever talked about besides personal issues. The time was 03:47 a.m. At that time, we had nothing much to talk about as our minds were oozing off, drunk with sleep.

"Aren't you tired?" was my question to her.

"I am, but I wish I wasn't," she replied.

"Well, I guess the Wi-Fi connection to your thoughts just dropped, so shall we call it a night".

"Haha, very funny, wait until it connects, you're going to get what you deserve... but I guess we should".

"Can you do me a favor though... maybe... just saying?"

"A Favor?... Okay, what is it? I am barely awake".

"Uhm... I don't know... maybe a picture of you".

"A picture? Really?... Okay, I'm flattered, I guess. But why now, can't sleep without thinking about me or something?" she forwarded a selfie of herself, "Don't expect much, I look like a zombie right now" she replied.

"Something like that I guess, just that you're pretty to think of," I said. My whole body trembled with joy after saying that statement, as I said something I didn't expect myself to ever say, or maybe my mind and brain were the ones who wrote it, and I was unconscious.

"Pretty? Me? You must be hallucinating from lack of sleep. But thanks, I think. You're making me blush over here... Or maybe that's just the screen glow. But anyway, go sleep, we can talk later".

"Goodnight then".

"Good night, may your dreams be filled with non-zombie versions of me".

She never took my request of asking for a picture as something that related to there being feelings. I spoke truth when I said she looked pretty, but a teasing she must have thought, one thing that brought us closer in mere seconds. She never thought about it much. Expressing my feelings to her was something that I really didn't know how to do, but it became that much simpler to do on the phone, but I loved every moment were my mind played a recollection of the tapes we call memories involving her, but it was too soon to tell her how I felt about her, for I've never met her in person. It was a virtual thing between me and her. During that night, the slumber was beautiful, which made me wake up late. I was greeted by the Saturday sunshine recalling it to be yellow. I spent the whole day watching movies, with frequent visitations of her in my mind, through the entire day I never picked up my phone to say let me text her or anything. Not only that, but I didn't want to seem clingy or that desperate or any other word that you might think of reader, she was a human too of course, she has other obligations outside just like how I had the ones of watching movies that day.

But I do have to ask you if you've ever noticed from time to time how the heart becomes so light when you're in love, you turn to see things with a different type of eye. We turn to see the feelings as a rainbow with no start nor ending but with the belief that a pot of gold lies at the end of the rainbow, with you being the start and that person being that pot of gold. We ended up not talking that day and that week as well, but I noticed a certain change in her bio, and yes, I was stalking her reader, it's not like you don't do it, and on his bio, I saw written words for a change. She has signed her name, and a few hobbies she likes and at the last line it was my name surrounded by hearts, two before and two after my name.

Chapter Six

In your mind reader, the picture is already painted perfectly, as you can see it clearly, that love was steaming in between Pearl and me. Though during that time, I didn't classify it as love, but I knew what feelings were, for it was my first time feeling that way, and I didn't know the certain mechanisms that drove those feelings. I didn't know much about word play to ooze her to make her mine, even now as we speak, I'm still clueless reader, believe it or not. My word play was in writing to express my feelings, that I knew very well, even though it felt like some words do not perfectly align and describe how I feel. Which button was I supposed to press, I was clueless, the same way you were with your first love. For no words of others you heard, only the words of the one who your heart beaten for were heard, even at times when they weren't available, you still remember your first "I love you" or "I love you too", and your first kiss, your first ever smile that was introduced by the scent of love from that person. Reader, I say even if that person has broken your heart to pieces and destroyed all the beliefs you had about love, the perfect image you had of falling in love, and being in love, you do still remember it. Love for the first time.

Another question if I may? Does positive thinking really bring about a positive lifestyle? They say with a positive mindset you will always bring about positivity in your life, as it attracts beauty, joy, and other relating things. Do you believe it?

Well, for the moment, for me, it was just a hypothesis with factors not considered, but during that time it felt like a theory build by the olden Greek constructors. For the joy that tranquilized my brain to think of her during the slumber showed effects of a positive aura, as days after talking to her, three guys in my class started talking to me, which was strange. I sat alone in class while other students were seated in two and three combining the desks together as friends, but I was the lonely outcast, but after getting acquainted with Pearl they started talking to me, and during free periods instead of doing my drawings, poems, and thinking to myself, they'd call me and converse about conspiracy theories, boy topics like girls, cars, homework, joke about each other, and other stuff. Reader, I know how you think, so don't go there, Pearl was for my heart and mind to talk about, not total strangers who seem to have been brought by a weird positivity flow.

From those three guys at the back of me, a group of guys who sat at the front far left corner started talking to me as well, but it was mostly a debate about the birthplace of science and hidden secrets, nothing more. With the three guys, Micheal, Christopher, and Jason, it went to a point whereby I was invited to eat with them during lunch, except for Jason, he didn't eat cafeteria food, you know the usual story, they serve jail food. I got introduced to their friends from different classes that they have lunch with, it was weird and all of it was happening fast. And of course, I just went with it because I wasn't a big NO person, except for reason, with that I can murder you with and give you a thousand reasons why I don't want to go hangout, instead of just saying "NO".

During that week, I spent most of my lunchtime eating with them outside the cafeteria, but still the cafeteria food, we just changed the seating. Talking and making a lot of jokes about teachers and each other, mostly themselves since they loved going to clubs, they will make expressions of what others were doing on the dance floor, how drunk they were, some drunk to a point where they were even dancing with our teachers and stuff. During that week, there was a girl who was dressed in Ravenswood Academy uniform who used to pass next to the road close to the fence of Crestwood, she seemed to be one of those students like Jason, who prefer going home during lunchtime to go eat and come back.

When she passed through the road, she used to pass us there eating as the road was a narrow passage like, no car would fit there, and the boys would act, as boys you know, stupid. They would call her, tease her and stuff, just as you know how boys do it. I too believe I should be inserted in that act of ridicule so, "we" would tease her, even though I never did, one rotten apple spoils them all as they say, so I too should be held accountable. It seemed that the girl passed through that road most of the time, I wasn't sure of it because it was my first time seeing her, and she seemed shy as the guys teased her. I only saw her for three days, then after that she disappeared, she must have gotten annoyed and changed roads to avoid the idiots at Crestwood which was us. I never knew that that girl would end up becoming my desire, wholeheartedly. But reader, we aren't there yet.

So, during that week I ended up making friends, and bullying a student who goes to Ravenswood Academy as it has always been a war zone, wherever Crestwood and Ravenswood met, through sports, students, academics, you mention it. It was a week that was confusing, as no word can express how it was.

Chapter Seven

When Friday greeted me with a smile, that shined so bright, it could blind me with its smile and happiness. I was able to rejoice in its spread of joy, absorbing the light to feed from it like a flower about to blossom. The aura surrounding me was so perfect it made me believe I could fly and conquer everything that would step in my way. The day was well spent at school, with the new friends I had, and loneliness started feeling like it's an old legend, folklore, a mythical creature that people talk about but doesn't exist. As I was now seeing myself fitting in with new friends, that little void inside of me was still available even though it wasn't felt all the time.

Every night before I went to sleep, I would watch Pearls photos, with my mind and heart arguing with each other that I should text her or call her because I missed her. The sad songs that I used to listen to started feeling like they were really sad songs, made for a person to cry. I started recalling the fact that I once said it, that it may be a two-minute thing that wasn't going to last, my heart cried with a melody of denial and provided reasons to oppose the statement uttered, promising to suffocate the lungs with my chest turning out to be heavy from time to time, but my mind was too hard-headed, it believed that it was so.

Friday approached, and during the night as I was listening to music while thinking about Pearl, I got a notification from her, just a little peek on my phone to find her name written on the screen my heart bounced with joy, with my lungs breathing in feelings that were supposedly being tossed out by my brain when my heart was mourning its own death in tears. I took my phone to check the message she has sent me it read;

"Hey... So, I was just sitting here, staring at my bookshelf, thinking about how boring my weekend is going to be, and then I thought, 'Hey, I know someone who might be able to make it less boring...' So, I just thought maybe you might like to meet up and grab a coffee or something? I just finished reading this creepy novel and I need someone to talk to about it. Oh, and I found this cool horror movie trailer that I think you'd love."

That was the moment where I realized that my heart's tears were feeling love, and my mind was just selfish. I should have listened to my heart instead of my brain and texted her.

"Hey... Uhm yeah, I guess I'd love to meet up with you, I guess", I responded.

"'I guess, I guess', you're really selling me on this meetup. Just kidding, I'm excited. And don't worry, I won't bite... unless you're into that sort of stuff. Oh, and by the way, I'll bring my book and horror movie trailer to share".

"Well, I was considering it to be like a lunch type of a thing, since you're a foodie and stuff".

"You remembered I'm a foodie? That's so sweet. Lunch sounds perfect, actually. There's this new sandwich shop I've been dying to try out. We could grab lunch there and then walk around the park? It's supposed to be nice out this Saturday, and yeah, I'm looking forward to it."

"Me too, I wanted to text you during the week, but I thought that you were too busy, so I didn't, even though I kind of missed talking to you".

"I missed talking to you too. I wasn't busy though, just got caught up in reading and stuff. But I'm glad you thought of me. It's been long."

"Yeah, it has, well let me try out some phrases to break the ice and start getting rid of this anxiety I have now".

"Aww, you're nervous! Well, go ahead and try out those phrases, I'm ready to be impressed. And don't worry, I'm feeling a little anxious too. But I know that as soon as we see each other, all that will melt away".

"Maybe, I guess, so see you tomorrow"

"Yes, Uhm see you tomorrow. I'll be the one with the big smile and nervous butterflies. Don't be late though. And uhm, yeah, I'm really looking forward to it. Goodnight, and sweet dreams."

On the text, it seemed like I wasn't interested anymore in talking to her, but the silence made was weird. When we were getting used to each other, everything just stopped in the middle and kind of gave me that little fade. We were both responsible for the little distance that caused that awkward moment, but the issue wasn't her but me, cause for me once you disappear from me, it's going to be hard to connect with you once you come back. That feeling that I had for you, it's going to be hard to reinstall it as it disappeared with you, a stranger you will become, and you alone will be left to try and reconnect it, it is hard to reconnect something that you don't know if it will last, that's why I lived it to her.

The next day approached with butterflies in my stomach as I prepared myself to go see her. I took a shower, dressed up and told my mother where I was going too, then took a taxi, and it delivered me to Elinor, and in the park, I searched for the shop that she was talking about, once found I went to wait for her in there. Five minutes passed which felt like eternity as people were staring at me seated alone not buying anything, well I'm not sure if they were staring at me, but it felt so. I took out my phone to call her and ask her where she was and as I dialed her number, I immediately got a call from her.

"Hey, where are you? I thought we were meeting up at the park? I'm already here, and I'm starting to think I got stood up?" she sounded a little bit concerned.

"I'm actually at the park, I was just about to call you and ask you where you were, I'm in the shop, Albert's Lunches and Munchies".

"Wait, what? You're at Albert's in Elinor? I thought we agreed to meet at The Springs Garden in Rutherford Hills. I'm already here, waiting for you... Not only that, but I'm starting to think we got our wires crossed?" she said with a little giggle.

"Wait", I was confused, "don't you live in Elinor?", sounding concerned.

She started laughing awkwardly, "Oh! I'm busted, I guess! Yeah, I don't live in Elinor but in Rutherford Hills. I just saw your bio written Crestwood the day you asked me where I was from, and though it would be a friendly conversation starter... I guess I got a little carried away", she tried speaking playful, but I could sense her voice shaking while trying to owe up to her mistake.

"Wait what...? You did not say that though..." I said disappointed and confused.

"Uhm, I mean... I didn't say that exactly. I just implied it, maybe? I don't know, I just got nervous and didn't want to scare you off, I guess. But I'm waiting for you at The Springs in Rutherford, and I promise to be honest from now on", sounding vulnerable.

"Uhm...you're really weird, but anyway, let me get a taxi then I'll be there in less than 15 minutes, okay?"

"Weird is my middle name! Okay, great, can't wait to see you! I'll meet you at the entrance. And don't worry, I promise to be on my best behavior... or at least, not too weird. See you soon!"

She sounded relieved that I was still willing to meet up with her, so I took a taxi to Rutherford, and it dropped me next to the entrance of The Springs, and there I saw her for the first time, short hair, white sneakers, black crop top, and blue jeans. When she saw me get out of the taxi she smiled and waved, gave me an awkward hug filled with nervousness from both sides.

"Hey! You made it! I was starting to think I'd have to send a search party. Love the... uhm... determined look on your face," she said as we both laughed. "And yeah, I chopped my hair, thought it was time for a change," she said trying to play it cool, while also excited and nervous.

"I didn't say anything," I said mesmerized.

"Well, you are staring... But anyway... how about we grab something to eat, I'm buying! I know this great spot is just around the corner from here. We can stuff our faces and then take a leisurely walk around The Garden. Sounds like a plan?".

We started walking in the shop's direction.

"I guess... so you just decided to be the gentlemen today and buy me food. Because I was supposed to do that, you know. You kind of destroying my style to exercise chivalry on you".

She chuckled, "Uhm, someone's got to make a good impression, right? Besides, I figured it's the least I can do after sending you up in Elinor."

I laughed while following her to the shop in silence, admiring her beauty, stealing her with my eyes, and trying to hide it.

"Stop... You're making me blush! You're going to turn me into a total softie," she said giggling and turning to hide her face. We arrived at the shop, entered, and sat down in a corner as I chose to, for I had to sit with my back facing everybody, and my face towards her. Not because of distractions or anything but eating in public places was one of the least favorite things I enjoyed doing but decided to do it just for her.

Chapter Eight

It was the first date, if I might call it that, first time seeing her, my veins were shaking like a snake basking in the sun. She was dazzling, and her beauty silenced my thoughts for I couldn't utter a word, even though I needed to construct words that will only perfectly make her smile, or chuckle, but her beauty silenced my thoughts, and the artists left as the inspiration laid in front of them was far more beautiful no pen would ink words to describe it, as they felt not worthy. As we were seated, she started admiring the shops' perfection and beauty, how she had been longing to try out one of the foods sold there. When she turned from admiring the place, she looked at me, with our eyes locking at the same interval, her eyes were sparkling as if pixie dust was used to make them. I was lost for a moment as she smiled and giggled, covering her smile with her hand, she pushed the menu forward to me and leaned back to her seat pulling her menu, asking me what I would like to have.

I snapped out of that hypnosis after the giggle, that she was laughing at me, I bowed my head and buried my face with the menu blushing. The waiter came to take our order, and she ordered a grilled chicken sandwich and an orange juice, and I ordered a roasted beef sandwich and a guava juice. As we waited for our order while being prepared, silence invited himself to our meet up, she tried to get rid of him by a little question asking me if I was mad at her, since she lied about the hole Elinor situation, and pretty much I wasn't mad, I was more keen to see this mysterious person that my heart had given in too.

"Hmm, so... here we are, finally meeting in person," she said while giggling nervously. She turned to look around and try to find something to talk about. "So uh, what do you think of this place?" smiling shyly.

We accidentally locked our eyes again, and she quickly looked away and started playing with the sugar packets on the table.

"It's nice, no wonder why it's filled with people, but I'm just shocked over the fact that you aren't talking too much at the moment, it's freaking me out, like a horror movie," I said blushing and chuckling.

"Oh, yeah... I know right? I'm usually the one who can't stop talking, but... I guess I'm just a little bit nervous, meeting you in person and all," she looked up in my eyes with hers sparkling with amusement. "But don't worry I'm sure the motor mouth will kick in soon enough. You might even be begging me to shut up by the end of the day," she said playfully rolling her eyes. "But between me and you, I'm just really happy that we are finally doing this. I was starting to think I'd never meet the person whose been putting up with my late-night rants and horror movie recommendations."

"Well, if I wasn't the one who was going to deplete that amount of energy you had when chatting, who was?"

"Oh, yeah... definitely the only one I know who can handle my excessive chatting and still manage to make me feel like I'm not boring you to tears," she smiled warmly and leaned in a bit closer. "And I have to say, I'm really glad it's you. I mean, who else would voluntarily go to Elinor, then track me down to Rutherford Hills, just to meet someone who's a talkative bookworm like me? You must be a glutton for punishment!"

"I guess, but I wanted to see you, so all obstacles had to be neglected, but I'm glad I came," I said trying to hide my sense of happiness.

The waiter brought our order while still in the conversation.

"Oh, perfect timing! Our foods here!" smiling at the waiter then turning back to me, with eyes sparkling with enthusiasm. "Okay so..." she picked up the sandwich and took a bite. "Mmm... this is so good!" chews and swallows. "I'm so glad we were sharing this experience together. Food always tastes better with good company, don't you think?" smiles warmly.

"Well, I assume it is if you don't chock," I said taking a bite of my sandwich.

She took a sip of juice and set the glass down, leaning in slightly, "So, now that we're eating, I have to ask. What's the verdict? Am I just as in person as I am over the phone," she said teasingly.

I took a bit on my sandwich to try and hide my blush, chewed, once composed I took a sip of my juice and said, "Well, I guess I have to admit that you look prettier in person than on the pictures you forwarded me, I think the camera was jealous when you were taking them cause it didn't show your true beauty, the beauty I see in front of I."

She started blushing deeply, looking down at her sandwich with a shy smile, "Oh stop! You're making me blush! But seriously, thank you...that means a lot to me." She took a bite of her sandwich trying to play it cool but couldn't help sneaking glances at me. "I have to say, you're pretty charming yourself, I mean, it takes a special kind of person to track me down from Elinor to Rutherford Hills, you must be determined one."

Reader, looks are not what the almighty has given me, even though I see mine as well suited for mine, I am grateful for the face I possess. That was just an exchange of pleasures.

"I mean I had too, I wanted to know you in person, the weirdness that came along with you, so we can be weird together," I said smiling.

"Exactly! Weirdos unite! I mean, who else can appreciate our quirky sense of humor and love for horror movies," playfully raising her sandwich in a toast, so I followed along raising mine to make a toast. "To being weird together, then! May our shared strangeness be the foundation of a beautiful friendship... or maybe something more."

"To being weirdos," we made a toast and continued eating our sandwiches.

"So, after we finish here, The Springs Garden awaits! But I want to show you something first before we head to the Springs."

"And that will be?" I asked with my face still buried in the sandwich.

"It's a surprise," she said with a mischievous look on her face.

We continued eating in silence, while stealing a glimpse of each other, locking eyes, smiling, and blushing like two shy little kids on a play date for the first time. Not knowing what words to use or what to say except to just laugh and smile, the warm feeling inside my heart was like a furnace, burning out with love and joy. It was beautiful. After eating we started preparing to leave.

"The Springs is one of my favorite places," she said as we stood up to departure from the shop. She was walking alongside me, feeling a sense of comfort and companionship. "Our detour is actually over there on the way to The Springs. There's a little path that leads to a beautiful spot... it's my favorite place to clear my head," she looked at me, with her eyes sparkling with excitement. She started walking in the direction of the path with the warmth of the sun on our skin, and the sounds of birds chirping in the distant trees like a movie scene, made to be caught by the eye. I followed her as she led on the path which opened up to a stunning view of The Springs, the water glistening in the sunlight with a few ducks in the water quacking, birds playing around the water, others building their houses around the lush grasses.

"Uhm, here we are! Isn't it breath taking?"

I turned my look from the scene to her, she was a little bit quiet, at peace I think, something that I couldn't described but only new that it's in existence only if you see it with your own eyes.

"I come here when I need to escape the world. It's sanctuary. And now, I got to show it to you," she said with her eyes still fixated on the view.

Chapter Nine

Silence, not making or accompanied by any sound is the definition that stands. Is it in purpose to be just like a ghost, shell out, only being felt by the presence of a mere cold breeze, a shadow in the dark, or a sound undefined by any other but the frequency fitted for it to be head. I spoke but never spoke, words were uttered but not out loud, so I gave her the opportunity for I was still analyzing her behavior, choice of words, body language, towards the words I may utter or just the body language in order for me to choose my words wisely. We stood there admiring the view, and she smiled feeling a sense of comfort and connection.

"I'm really glad we're doing this; it feels like we've known each other for a long time. This place is special to me and I'm happy to share it with you."

She took a step back, putting some space between us, but still fixated on the view. She continued walking along the path to get closer to get a better view of the place, and I followed the leader like a scout. As we were walking along the path, I noticed something on Pearl that I've never seen before. Something that seemed to have been there for a long time, but was hidden so well that I couldn't see, not in her pictures nor even now as we are on this so-called date. I get that all aspects were noticeable, like the fact that Pearl was hairy, and I like that or to rephrase that, I loved that about her, and reader on this note I have to ask, why do hairy girls like shaving their legs and arms to look like they have hairless skin? Why choose to shave, for beauty can never be represented as a unit, but has to differ so as perfection?

I noticed scars on her wrist, which I couldn't help but stare at and wonder how is it possible for a girl like her to have those scars on her arm, and how did I miss it. She instinctively covered her wrist, with the anticipation that she must have seen me gazing at it, a fleeting look of vulnerability crossed her face.

"Oh, Uhm, yeah...I got those in an accident a while ago."

She said quickly trying to brush it off, it seemed I've laid eyes on something that I wasn't supposed to see. She forced a smile and tried to change the subject but I was too busy lost in my thoughts trying to figure out what could be the reason for them, but only made it worse as she started walking fast, holding her wrist from time to time which made him trip over a rock and she merely fell but caught her.

"You know...it's okay. I get that I'm Prince Charming, that's why you're tripping so much," I said teasing her trying to get her to feel at ease.

She laughed, looking relieved that I wasn't making a big deal out of the scars, "Oh, shut up! Prince Charming, huh?" she said playfully rolling her eyes. "Well, I suppose I did trip into your arms literally, I'm just a little bit awkward sometimes," she shrugged looking down at her feet, she looked up at me, a mischievous glint in her eyes. "But hey, at least I'm consistent right? So, Prince Charming, what's your next move? Going to sweep me off my feet, again?" teasingly raising her eyebrow.

"Well, I guess we have to find out when we reach the spot, then you'll see," I said teasing.

"Ah, the spot!", she slapped her head gently as she seemed to have forgotten where we were going. "Yes, let's go find it, I promise it's worth the trip."

We started walking again, with her leading the way, and after a few minutes of walking we stopped at a beautiful overlook.

"Ta-da! What do you think?" she said spreading her arms wide gesturing to the stunning view.

The overlook offered a breathtaking panorama of the surrounding landscape, with rolling hills and towering trees as far as the eye can see. It was one of those views in which you would wish you could stop time and live in the moment for eternity. It was peaceful like the air was newly made, with perfection the smell of serenity. Like the saying of riding into the sunset, I would chase this heaven for a lifetime. As I was admiring the view, by a sense of just breathing in the beauty, the tranquility, the moment, I turned to look at her and she smiled, looking at me with a sense of pride and happiness.

"I come here when I need to clear my head or feel inspired. It's my slice of heaven," she sat down on a nearby rock, patting the space beside her. "Want to seat and take it in for a bit?"

Reader, if I may, why is it that most of the time when we turn to be in a peaceful place, all the words we have get eradicated, and the voices in your mind, if you have some, become silent? It's like that moment opens up this new version, this type of being that you've never considered to live inside of you. Through that moment, time becomes the enemy to that being and as you wish for time to stop it turns to run faster than clock. The weirdest part about that is that we turn to forget the feeling of that peace, that little heaven on earth, and even if you've taken pictures or videos, they themselves are not convincing enough to explain that feeling. Why is peace so forgettable once you have had a taste of it? Strange.

When Pearl patted the rock to come seat with her, I did so, while still stunned by the view.

"Well, I guess it is true..." I spoke.

She smiled following my gaze out at the view, "What's true?" she said, curious, turning to face me, our legs touching slightly as we sat together on the rock, a comfortable silence settling between us, waiting for me to continue, her eyes sparkling with interest.

"Well, like how many mythological creatures do you know of, and how many are there exactly. I mean we've grown up with so many fascinating folklore's that we just believed that they are just old tales, but looking at this place... it kind of gives me that weird vibe that if sirens were real, they'll chose to live here." I turned and looked at her, "like mermaids really do exist, and this is your place huh? little mermaid," I said smiling. "I mean what other reason would it be, for you to find peace here and keep it to yourself?" I began laughing.

She laughed, playfully rolling her eyes, "Oh, you're such a goofball! Mermaids, really? But I guess this place does have a certain magical feel to it, doesn't it?" she said gazing out at the view, a faraway look in her eyes, then turned back to me, with a sly grin spreading across her face. "And I suppose I do feel a connection to the water... and the mysteries that lie beneath the surface," she winked, leaning in, a conspiratorial whisper escaping her lips. "But don't tell anyone, I wouldn't want to ruin my reputation as a mere mortal," she giggled, with the sound carried away by the gentle breeze. I joined in with laughter and the sound was echoing through the overlook, she then began wiping tears from her eyes, still chuckling, "Oh, I needed that, thanks for sharing in the silliness with me!" Then she gazed at me, with her eyes shining with warmth and friendship. The moment stretched out, comfortable and peaceful, as we were seated together, taking in the beauty of the overlook and each other's company.

"You know, it's really nice here, the breeze, the view and you," I began hesitating in uttering more of the words, "but... can I be honest with you?" I spoke.

She smiled softly, nodding encouragingly, "Of course, you can be honest with me. I want to hear what's on your mind," she leaned in slightly, attention focused on me, a gentle expression on her face, inviting me to open up and share my feelings, if only butterflies were to be uttered out my lips. I couldn't dare to face her for what I was about to say, turned my face and fixated my gaze on the view with hope for the breeze to direct my words.

"The scars on your wrist are from a razor blade, and they are still visible because it's believed that these scars are a reflection of the emotional scars that you have... and they are connected. The slow fading of the scars is seen as a symbol of the enduring nature of emotional pain, and the idea that true healing requires more than just a physical recovery," I said fixated on the view.

Stunned, silence fell between us, the only sound being the gentle rustling of the leaves in the breeze. She slowly turned her face to me, her eyes welling up with tears, a mix of emotions flashing across her face - shock, vulnerability and a sense of fear resulted. She took a deep breath, her voice barely above a whisper, " How did you...?" she paused, collecting her thoughts, "I didn't think anyone could tell. I've tried to hide them, to keep them concealed." She looked down, her gaze fixed on her wrist as if seeing the scars for the first time. A single tear rolled down her cheek, and she quickly wiped it away, trying to compose herself.

Now, reader, with my gaze fixated on the view, it did not prevent me from witnessing the emotional turmoil that approached her. It is known that the human eyes have a wide field of view, allowing us to see objects outside of our direct line of sight, namely called the peripheral vision. The ability to see things on either side of us without directly looking at them and having both eyes allows us to see a wider field of view than only one eye. Our brains combine the images from each eye to create a single, wider view. Even when focusing on something directly in front of us, our eyes make small, involuntary movements, which help us take in more information from our surroundings. With Pearl seated next to me, with me fixated on the view, didn't not mean I turned a blind eye on the emotions that floated around her, I did take notice of them. With that being so, I turned to look at her and noticed tears up in her eyes, and her tears stirred mine and water started building up in my eyes, but I couldn't allow a waterfall to be forged on my face, I said to her.

"You know if you want to share, I'm here for you right?... And if you are not ready it's also fine... I know the feeling... " I grabbed her hand. "Cause I've also been in that situation too, but... mine don't actually last long, and aren't that dark and bold like yours, they seem like they've been there for a while," wiped the tear from her face.

A look of surprise crossed her face, followed by a deep sense of gratitude. She smiled weakly, her eyes welling up again, took a deep breath, letting it out slowly, "I've carried this burden for so long, trying to hide it from everyone. But seeing that you've been through something similar... it gives me hope. Maybe I can finally let go of some of this pain." She said wiping away her tears, her voice cracking, turning to look at me with a sense of wonder, "Your scars don't last long? What do you mean?" leaning in, her eyes locked on mine, searching for answers and a connection, her hand instinctively reaches out as if to touch my arm, but hesitates, unsure if she should. I reached out, pulled her hand closer to my arm, and pulled my long sleeve shirt showing her my wrist with lines that seemed to be fading away.

She gasped softly, her eyes widening in surprise, "Oh... they are fading, just like you said," gently touching my wrist, tracing the faint lines with her fingers, she looked up at me, a mixture of emotions on her face - amazement, curiosity, and a deep sense of connection, "How did you... overcome it?" asking softly, her voice filled with a sense of longing.

"Uhm... I think it's the amount of things that I do, I don't know... I guess," I turned my gaze from her and looked at my feet hanging on the rock. "I guess, everything that I do turns to redirect my mind from thinking too much about the pain I feel, the poetry, music, drawing, watching movies and cartoons, and listening to music, I guess, we treat it differently, I think."

But to be honest, reader, today as I write this, the serenity that I felt when I was listening to music for hours drawing, is no longer my tranquility. The poems I used to write to express myself, a visitation I only make from time to time to dust the papers and bookshelf of my mind, sometimes change and clean the pipe that holds the ink of my pen as it solidifies, as it remains unused, I turn to write a few words, but never get the heart to finish what I've written. I still listen to music, just to drift away to my own world, a world better than this one, and with the movies I only watch comedy and animation only. I have grown a fear deep inside of me that boils fire that I have to extinguish every time a movie or series turns to those lovey dovey scenes, my heart burns, my chest pains, my eyes swells, my brain aches. I fear the gaze of love, for it seems to be my death. It's funny how I say lovey dovey based on how I feel, to put in mind, a reminder that love was worthied by I, now I seek no intention nor desire for it to cross my line of sight.

Chapter Ten

Sharing. Emotions are kind of hard-to-understand reader, not in the case of others for I speak for I and I alone. Listening to a person expressing their feelings to another is magical, it's beautiful, it amazes me to listen to others share the good or bad their heart holds, but in the case of I sharing it's hard. I sometimes feel like a lot of people can have the idea of what listening can be, but to construct it its hard, for once I even got a complement from SpongeBob that I should've studied psychology for it lives inside of me, to listen, observe, analyze and construct.

The idea of a home resembles the feeling of there being people to listen to you, not assume, not judge, or control you including giving advice were not necessary, but just be there to lend an ear. I guess that what's she found in me, most people find in me, but my search for a home, a person to listen to me, still stretches miles and miles away from me, so I lay in silence. When I'm sharing, I turn to say a lot, and some of the important facts which are required to be noted are missed and I turn to bore those lending an ear. Sometimes I turn to say less, but still don't untangle the knots my heart has made with my veins, a lot of emotions can result not just anger or pain. That's why I still say silence isn't silent. The expression was laid, and words were uttered reader, and she pulled her hand back, but not before giving my wrist a gentle squeeze stating that she was glad that I got to show her, and it gave her hope that maybe in due time he might heal as well. But her smile was weak, and her eyes were still shining with tears.

So, she took a deep breath, as if stealing herself, "I think I'm ready to talk about it now. About what happened, and how I got those scars." Paused, looking at me for support and encouragement, "Will you listen?"

"Well... you've always been a radio so broadcast away."

She laughed, a bright smile spreading across her face, "Oh, you're such a goofball! Always a radio huh?" playfully rolling her eyes. She took another deep breath, settling in to share her story. "Okay DJ, turn up the volume, I'm ready to broadcast my secrets," smiles, trying to hide her nerves. Then began to speak, her voice was barely above whisper,

"It started a few years ago, when I was going through a tough time. I felt lost, alone, and like I had no control over my life. I was struggling with some dark emotions, and one day I found myself in a moment of desperation, and I... I hurt myself." She looked down, her voice cracking, she took a moment to compose herself, then continued.

"It was a cry for help, I think. A way to cope with the pain I was feeling inside. But it only led to more pain, more scars, and more secrets," she sighed, her eyes locked on mine, searching for understanding and acceptance.

"But seeing your scars, knowing that you've been through something similar... it gives me hope that I'm not alone, and that maybe, just maybe, I can heal too."

I took her hand and tilted it to get a glimpse of her wrist, "And you're still doing it, because there's are fresh wounds," I said tracing the fresh scar with my finger carefully. Her eyes dropped, and she pulled her hand away, trying to cover the fresh wound.

"Oh... I ..." she paused and took a deep breath. Looked up in my eyes, tears welling up in her eyes again.

"You're right, I am still struggling. It's not something I can stop doing overnight. It's a... a coping mechanism, I guess. A way to deal with the pain and emotions that still linger inside me." She sighed, feeling a mix of shame and vulnerability, a sign for me to cease my mind from generating questions. I pulled her closer to me and gave her a hug.

"You know, if you ever want to talk, I'm here for you, okay?"

She wrapped her arms around me, holding me tightly, "Thank you", smiled softly, with a sense of comfort and support. Then pulled back slightly, looking up at me and squeezed my hand.

"I'm glad you're here for me"

"Yeah, you know... you kind of look gorgeous when you cry, your eyes sparkle like marbles," I said teasing her.

She blushed looking down, trying to hide the smile," Oh stop it. You're making me blush," she looked up at me, with her eyes sparkling with amusement "Marbles huh? I'll take as a complement. You're such a charmer, aren't you? Trying to distract me from my tears with sweet talk!" she said playfully rolling her eyes, she held her gaze, her expression softening.

"Thanks for being here."

We remained seated there for hours in silence admiring the beauty of the place, taking it in, piece by piece. After hours of silence, she turned to me, with a curious expression asked," What are you thinking about? You've been quiet for a while" leaned in slightly, interested in my thoughts. Her hand inches closer to mine, as if seeking a gentle, comforting touch.

"I don't know what I'm thinking, my mind is just blank at the moment", fixated on the view, what was there to think of, for peace has laid itself in front of my eyes and shut the mind up to just live in the moment.

"That's okay. Sometimes the best moments are the ones where we don't need to think. We can just... be" she said smiling. She gently took my hand which caused me to turn away from the view and gaze at her with a smile, her touch was warm and comforting. "Let's just enjoy the silence, then. And the beauty surrounding us," squeezing my hand softly, a sense of calm and connection following between us. With a mischievous look and a smirk, I turned away with a little bit of a side eyes.

"But..."

Curiosity introduced himself to her look, "But?" she said smiling softly. Her hand still holding mine, she leaned in slightly, as if anxious to hear my thoughts. "What is it? You can tell me," Her voice barely above a whisper, creating a sense of intimacy and trust to think.

"Well... I still want to hear you talk, it's freaking me out that the talkative Pearl that I know is you, it's weird and freaky," I said with a chuckle.

She laughed, with a warm, and gentle sound, "Oh! I'm sorry about that! I think I just got caught up in the moment and didn't want to break the silence, or maybe nervous or something," she smiled with her eyes sparkling. "But don't worry, I'm still here, and talkative. I just needed a little break from talking, that's all. I promise I won't turn into a quiet, mysterious person on you!" leaning in with a conspiratorial look on her face and smiled.

Time flew past, as the sunset was starting to paint the sky with hues of yellow and orange, adding a dash of glitter on top. Darkness became exhausted of listening to the sun talk about a beautiful star that resided on earth, keen to see, he approached fast. We watched with awe as the planet seemed to absorb the colors, turning the leaves to shimmer with a soft, ethereal light. As if all the plants were drinking the beauty of the sky, the beauty of the sunset. With Pearl on my side, she turned to me, her face aglow with the fading light.

"I'm glad we got to experience this together. It feels like a special moment, one that we'll remember long after the sunset fades."

"Yeah, I guess, but my favorite part was to see the only beauty that lies next to me, no beauty of worlds can neutralize such tranquility I gaze at."

"I feel the same way about you. You're the beauty that I see, the tranquility that I feel, when we're together. You make me feel seen, and appreciated and loved... just for who I am."

We remained there watching the sunset, to give darkness a glimpse of the star that resided on earth, a few moments. It saw with its own eyes, delighted with a shooting star it waved to acknowledge, or maybe it must've been a satellite who knows but hey. Once acquainted with darkness to keep us shining, I jumped off the rock and assisted her in getting down, held her hand and walked back to the Spring Garden entrance to take a taxi back home. We passed through the park as we walked in silence, her head lay on my shoulder. As we reached the gate, she let go, a taxi was called.

"Let me know you've arrived safe," she said.

"Will do"

"Goodbye"

"Goodbye" we hugged.

Upon my arrival at home, I confirmed my safe arrival with her. With delight she was glad to have arrived and to spend the day with her.

Chapter Eleven

In question, you may ask yourself why I didn't kiss her on the shorts that were open, the amount of times she gazed in my eyes, locked, feeling a sense of connection.

Why didn't I?

In truth I was scared, trembling to be precise. In humanity the timing wasn't right, for a lot of emotions were felt during that time and being expressed. I couldn't nor will ever use someone's emotions to get something that I desire, its selfish and wicked. It's not what love is.

The concept of using someone's emotions for your desire is sickening, even though in this generation it is considered. Thats why you'll find out next time when you try to make a move on that person, he or she will respond by telling you that what happened between the two of was a mistake, they were down low and vulnerable and weren't thinking straight. If they say that, what are you going to say or feel, remember you can't argue with someone's feelings, even worse knowing that that wasn't right. But if you can and have all the answers reader, well I guess you deserve an Oscar.

Instead of what could've happened or what should've happened I was none-the-less glad to have spent the day with her. Which resulted in bringing us even closer together than we ever were. As days went by, we spent most time calling each other, texting on Facebook became something else for me, I had her, so I needed nothing else including the app. We spent most time talking about the boys she dated before, how she kind of has a thing for bad boys, troubled past, those who walked around with pocket knives, and to put it on note, I'm not that kind of a person, the red pocket knife I had when I was young I threw it away cause it has no use except to weigh a lot in my pocket as we pretended to be gangsters, if it were coins then yes but a knife, useless. We started engaging about the scars going into deeper details about the causes for them, from the scars to childhood memories, it was dazzling listening to her laugh, yelling at her nephews and nieces to leave her room and stop beating each other up. Reader, never call a person when baby-sitting unless if you're really looking forward to laughing your brains out, best memory. It was awesome knowing Pearl. After weeks of communication, we planned another get together or as you might call it, a "date". But this time it was going to be a picnic in Elinor, where me and her are going to watch a movie together on a PC since there weren't any cinemas around our places.

Chapter Twelve

I once asked a question reader, feel free to engage, that why is it that when girls like a person they prefer not to say anything. I mean signs are there like eye contact, the unnecessary laugh of unfunny jokes, the walking together so close like you're now a thing, a couple but not. Why is it that girls can't just approach guys and genuinely tell them how they feel? Instead of waiting for the guy to say something first, or to fall for someone else then get angry and shun them. I once asked my high school crush that question, and her respond was that guys must learn to men up because they are soon going to be the head of the house, family, and the women will be the second in command. What is your perspective on that, I can provide mine but it's going to be less fun, but a girl who would approach me and tell me that she feels a certain way, I won't judge, feelings are weird to understand. And everyone should feel free to express them I guess, even though I don't very much but you should.

I planned that before the end of the year to tell Pearl how I felt about her, and the picnic idea was one step in my goal of making her my girlfriend. When the June holidays hit us, all I had to do was to put it in phase and so I did. On a Friday night I texted her with simple pleasure;

"Hey, you busy," I texted.

"Reading and waiting for you to text me off-course, its Friday," she replied. It was a routine, to call each other on the weekends and on weekdays we would do normal stuff like focus on school and stuff.

"Okay I texted, and I wanted to ask if you're free tomorrow?"

"I was totally free tomorrow! I mean, I had plans to read a book and watch some movies, but I can totally reschedule those for... something more exciting! Got something in mind?"

"Well, I know it's a little bit of a short notice, but I was wondering if we could meet up at the park in Elinor and have a little picnic type of a movie or something?"

"Short notice? Don't worry about it! I'm always up for a spontaneous adventure! Plus, I've got a blanket and a basket ready to go... I just need to grab some snacks, and we're all set! What time were you thinking? And what movie did you have in mind? I'm so down for rom-com or a horror movie... or really anything as long as it's with you."

"Well, I was thinking of around 13:00 and then the movie, maybe Scary Movie 1."

"Great choice, classic blend between horror and comedy, that means I'll meet you at the park entrance at 12:55 so we can set up our little picnic spot. Brings drinks and I'll add something cozy in case it gets chilly."

"Alright."

"I'm so excited! This is going to be epic."

"Yeah, I can't wait."

"Counting hours, I should probably get some sleep now, so I'm not a zombie tomorrow... but I know I'll be too excited to sleep! Tomorrow."

"Tomorrow?"

"It's a date! I'll be dreaming of our picnic movie day tonight... and probably talking to myself about how excited I am! Goodnight, and sweet dreams!"

"Night"

She might have called it a date but it's the one you're thinking of, define date; a social or romantic appointment or engagement. You can choose your word reader, and I chose social, so we were going to socialize reader. When the morning sunrise clocked on the chicken's watch to start clucking, I was already up. All that was required was to prepare myself and hit the road, which I did.

I arrived at the gate of the park and a little distance far away, I saw her setting up a little picnic spot. As I approached a blanket was spread out, snacks arranged. She was wearing a yellow sundress with white flowers, her hair tied up in a ponytail with a few loose strands framing her face, she had on a huge smile on her face.

"Hey!", she exclaimed, running up to me for a big hug. "I'm so glad you're here! I've been waiting for what feels like forever." I wasn't late, I arrived exactly at the time planned, but it seemed like she came in a little bit early.

I chuckled, "I had to share a taxi, my bad, but you look particularly splendid if I'd say. The night hasn't turned you into a zombie yet."

"Thank you for the compliment! And no, the night didn't turn me into a zombie, but I did have a hard time sleeping because I was too excited for today!" she said as we walked to the picnic spot, she took her arm and snuggled it in close. We arrived at the blanket, and she gestured for me to sit down. "Welcome to our little setup! I brought your favorite snacks, and I even made some sandwiches." We exchanged food, handed me the sandwich and drinks plus snacks, had a little chat while eating trying to catch up on how our week was and how we were going to spend the school holidays.

"So, are you ready for the scary movie?" she asked, grinning mischievously.

"Uhm...well, before that... I have to say I know we were supposed to watch Scary Movie 1, but uhm..." I said squinting my face. Her eyes widened in surprise. "I brought a different movie," I took out my PC from my bag and showed her a picture of the cover.

"Oh my gosh, The Fault in Our Stars! I love this book! And the movie is so beautiful, but also heart-wrenching!" taking my PC from me and gazing at the cover. "I wasn't expecting this, but I'm so glad you brought it! I've been wanting to watch this movie again," smiling up at me, with a hint of shyness.

"Well, I am a gentleman after all," I said teasing.

She giggled, "Aww, a gentleman, huh? Well, I'm impressed, Mr. Chivalrous!" settling in closer to me, getting cozy. "Okay, gentleman, let's watch this movie together then. I'll try to hold back my tears, but no promises!"

Starting the movie, and snuggling up close, we both sat in comfortable silence, watching the movie together with the sun shining down on us, casting a warm glow over our little picnic setup. As the movie played, she occasionally kept glancing over at me, smiling at my reactions to the story at the emotional moments, she snuggled in closer, feeling comfortable and safe beside me. Time passed, and we were both absorbed in the world of Hazel and Augustus, a sudden tear rolled down her cheek, and she quickly wiped it away. I noticed it and paused the movie, turning to her.

"Tears, explain," I said with a warm smile.

She looked up at me, feeling a bit embarrassed, "Uhm... it's the movie," she said with a trembling voice. "It's so beautiful, but also heartbreaking. I can't help but feel for the characters. But it's not just the movie, being here with you, feeling so comfortable and happy... it's just really special to me."

"Ahh, now you're going to make me cry," I stood up took two steps in front of her while she was still sitting down, and screamed, "Composure! Composure! Dimpho Composure!" and went back to sit down and pretended as if I didn't do that.

She burst out laughing at my sudden outburst and dramatics, "Haha, oh my gosh, you're such a goofball!" she said, wiping away tears of laughter. She shook her head, grinning at me. "Composure, Dimpho composure?" she teased, chuckling. "I think you lost that for a second there!" playfully rolling her eyes and snuggling back into our cozy picnic setup. "But I have to admit, it's pretty adorable when you try to be tough but can't hide your emotions," giving a sly smile.

"Hey, hey, hey!" I turned to her with a side eye and a smirk. "I am a man, Pearl! I am a man, I am not trying to be tough, I am tough," I said flexing my skinny biceps.

She burst out laughing again, unable to contain herself, "Oh, okay Mr. Men!" teasing and giggling. "I see those scrawny biceps and I'm shaking in my boot!" then started poking me as I flexed, chuckling at the sight. "Skinny biceps, but a heart of gold, I'm sure," she said with a grin, leaning in close, still smiling. With my side eye glance, I turned to the PC, pressed resume to continue watching the movie. The movie's emotional moments started to unfold again, and we were both invested in the story. She reached out and gently took my hand, giving it a soft squeeze. "This is such a beautiful movie," she whispered, her eyes fixated on the screen.

"Hush, no noise in the cinema, you're disturbing others," I said pointing at the trees and the birds.

She giggled and pretended to zip her lips shut, making a "silent" gesture with her fingers, "Shh, okay, okay! I'll be quiet, cinema police!" then nodded towards the trees and birds, playing along with the joke. "Yes, we wouldn't want to disturb the other patrons... like squirrels and the leaves," she stifled a grin and focused on the movie again, but kept sneaking glances at me, enjoying the lighthearted moment. I couldn't help but release a mischievous silly chuckle, and she tried to stifle her laugh, but it was no use. We started laughing, and we both sat there, trying to be quiet but unable to contain our laughter. The movie continued to play, but we were not paying attention anymore, too caught up in our own little moment of silliness. She wiped tears away from her eyes, and we exchanged a look of pure joy and connection. Then in a moment our focus turned to increase when the movie reached the part where Augustus had a breakdown when going to buy a pack of cigarettes. It felt her squeezing my hand gently, feeling a sense of empathy for the characters.

"Augustus's vulnerability is so raw and honest... it's heartbreaking to see him struggle like this," glanced at me to see how I'm reacting to the scene. "How about you? What are you thinking right now?"

"Uhm... I don't know actually?" I whispered still fixated on the movie.

"Thats okay, just be present in the moment," she whispered, her eyes also fixated on the screen. She let go of my hand, allowing me to fully immerse myself in the scene. The silence between us was comforting, a shared experience connecting us as we watched. I felt a lump on my throat when Augustus invited Hazel to his funeral.

"Oh, man... this part always gets me," she whispered, her voice cracking slightly. She reached for my hand again, seeking a connection as we experienced the poignant moment together. "Augustus desires to leave a lasting impact on Hazel, to be remembered... it's beautiful and heartbreaking at the same time." She glanced at me, and in my eyes, tears were welling up. "We're both crying now Mr. Tough Guy," she whispered smiling softly.

"Yeah uhm... allergies, you're the one crying here," I said with a cracking voice.

"Oh, Okay, allergies, sure!" she teases, laughing through her tears. "Keep telling yourself that Tough Guy. But I know you're feeling the feels too."

"Shut up!" I said with a chuckle.

We watched the movie in silence until the credits rolled, and we remained seated in comfortable silence for a moment, processing the emotional journey we just experienced. She finally broke the silence, speaking softly, "That was beautiful. I'm so glad we watched it together. What did you think about the ending? Did it resonate with you?"

"I don't know honestly, I don't know..." I paused for a moment "what about you?"

"For me, the ending was bittersweet. Happy and sad, all mixed together. It felt real, like life."

"But honestly, just to state this, i think most people who have gone under a lot of trauma or lifelong illnesses and stuff value love and life more than all of us who haven't experienced those types of tragedies, that why we care less about them nor even value them, we turn to value them when it's too late or when the world no longer favors us, don't you think?"

"Absolutely, I think you're right. People who have faced significant challenges, trauma, or adversity often develop a deeper appreciation for life and love. They understand the fragility and beauty of existence in a way that others might not. It's as if they've been given a second chance, a new perspective, or a deeper understanding of what truly matters. They learn to cherish every moment, every connection, and every breath." She looked at me, locked eyes, "You know, I think that's one of the most beautiful things about the human spirit, the capacity to find strength, resilience, and love in the face of adversity."

"Yeah, couldn't have said it better, all the movies like Clouds, Five Feet Apart, The In Between and After, even though it sucks."

She looked at me with a side eye, "I'll forgive you for saying that" she chuckled.

I shrugged and smiled, reaching for a bag of chips, "They're just weird I guess," I said with a voice filled with a mix of amusement and curiosity.

Chapter Thirteen

After talking about the movie, I ate a few chips and laid my back on the blanket staring at the blue sky underneath the leaves of the tree that shaded us. She joined in gazing up at the sky, her voice relaxed and content, "Ahh, this is the life... good movie, good snacks, and even better company. What more could we ask for?" she turned her face to me, a lazy smile spreading across her face. "You know, I love days like this. No rush, no fuss... just enjoying the moment," her eyes drifted back to the sky, watching the leaves rustling gently in the breeze. "It's like the world is reminding us to slow down and appreciate the little things," she paused, taking a deep breath of fresh air, "What's on your mind? You seem lost in thought?"

"If I'm lost, then you found me," I laughed. "The day is nice but wait until the school holidays bid us goodbye... the amount of schoolwork."

She nodded sympathetically, understanding the impending doom of schoolwork, "Ugh, don't remind me! School holidays flying by is like a ticking time bomb, isn't it? One minute we're chilling, the next we're drowning in assignments and exams," she sat up, leaning on her elbow, and turned to face me. "But let's not think about that right now. Let's just enjoy the moment, this nice day and each other's company. We can worry about school later," she smiled mischievously.

"Yeah, I guess, so what's on your mind, you like asking me that question a lot, now it's your turn, what's on your mind, do tell," I said smiling, smitten.

She laughed, "Alright, alright, I deserved that," she said with a grin. "I guess I was just trying to distract myself from my own thoughts," she paused collecting her thoughts before sharing. "To be honest, I've been thinking about the future a lot lately. What we want to do after school, where we want to go, that kind of thing." She glanced at me, curious, "I know we've talked about it before, but I feel like we're getting closer to having to make some real decisions. It's exciting but a bit scary, you know?" She leaned back on the blanket, looking up at the sky again. Now reader on this part, I wasn't sure whether she was talking about us, or generally school issues or as individuals, but I took it with the last one. "I guess I'm just wondering about what the future holds and hoping we can figure it out together."

"But you already planned everything though, you shouldn't be scared. The future holds things that you are working for now, but if you aren't working on them, you should start getting scared. Like for me, the only thing that scares me is that will I live fully enough to see it, or am I working on something that's going to be just cut short?"

"I see what you mean. I guess I have planned and dreamt, but that doesn't mean I'm not afraid of the unknown," she sat up, her eyes locking in mine. "And your fear... that's a tough one. It's like we're always told to make the most of the time we have, but what if that time is shorter than we think?" she took a deep breath, her voice filled with conviction. "But here's the thing; we can't control the length of our lives, but we can control how we live them. We can choose to make every moment count, to chase our dreams, and to never give up." She reached out, placing a reassuring hand on my arm, "And I promise you, no matter what life throws our way, we'll face it together. We'll make the most of every moment, and we'll live life to the fullest."

"I guess, creepy lady," I said teasing.

She feigns offense, clutching her heart dramatically, "Creepy lady? Creepy lady?! I'll have you know, I'm charming and a sophisticated individual... with a hint of mystery and intrigue, of course." She winked, grinning mischievously, leaned in, a conspiratorial whisper escaped her lips. "Creepy lady, maybe I should start a club... or a cult. Muahahaha!"

"Hell nah," I took the blanket we were wearing, and threw it over her head covering her whole body and began tickling her.

"Ahhhh!" flails and squirms under the blanket, "Oh no, Oh no! Not tickles! Anything but the tickles!" She tried to escape, but I was too quick. "Okay, Okay! I surrender!" giggling uncontrollably, "You win! You win!" Took a deep breath, trying to compose herself. "You're going to pay for this, just you wait!" she peeked out from under the blanket, eyes sparkling with mischief. She tried to grab me, but I dodged and weaved, still tickling her "Ahhhh! Stop! Stop!" laughing hysterically.

"Promise no evil stuff first!" I said laughing while still tickling her.

"I promise to behave and be kind! No tickle torture or sneak attack, I swear!" she held her hands up in a peaceful gesture, and I let her go.

"Good" I got back to lying down while laughing at her and she joined on the blanket lying down beside me. We gazed up at the sky together, watching the clouds drift lazily by. The warm sun shining down on us, casting a cozy glow over the moment. She turned to me smiling softly, "You know, sometimes it's nice to just relax and enjoy the simple things in life... like the beautiful day, good company, and a comfy blanket." She closed her eyes, feeling the warmth and contentment wash over her. After a few minutes of lying there in silence, the peaceful afternoon was interrupted by her phone ringing. She sighed, reluctantly getting up from the blanket.

"Hey, sis! What's up?" she answered, trying to sound cheerful despite the interruption. She listened for a moment, nodding as if she could see her.

"Okay, Okay! I'll be right over. Love you!"

She hung up the phone and turned to me, apologetic. "Sorry, I've got to run! My sister needs me. But let's catch up again soon, maybe we can plan something for next week?" She started getting her things, feeling a bit disappointed. "Uhm... Okay clean up here when you go okay. Rain check on the chill time?"

"Sure, thing... good looking," I said teasing her.

She grinned, feeling a bit flattered but pleased, "Hey, watch it! I'm not just a pretty face, you know!" she teased back laughing. "But thanks, I guess." She blew a playful kiss my way. "Later, handsome!

Don't forget about me while I'm off to saving the day for my sis!" With her heading off, a bit energized from the banter. I sat there alone for a couple of hours, taking in the afternoon until the sun was ready to say goodbye. My phone rang, with a notification popping on my lockscreen with Pearls name shining in bold italic.

"Hey! Are you home? What's up? I just got back from my sisters and I'm relaxing. Wanted to say hi and see what you're up to."

"Hey, I'm still at the park, watching the sunset and thinking," I replied.

"Aww, that sounds lovely! Enjoying the sunset and your thoughts. I'm a bit jealous. Wish I was still there with you. What's on your mind? Anything deep or just soaking in the moment."

"Just thinking about someone talkative."

"Hmm, talkative, huh? Someone specific or just a general observation? And are you finding this talkative person endearing or exhausting?"

"Endearing, she always leaves a question mark in my mind, I don't know why, mysterious, and creepy like the horror movies she likes."

"Haha, I think I know who the talkative mystery girl might be! I'm flattered to be considered endearing, even if I do leave you with unanswered questions. And yeah, I guess my love for horror movies can be a bit... unsettling at times. But hey, it's all a part of my charm."

"Yeah, I guess it is pretty girl."

"You're making me blush. I think we've got a good thing going here – a little mystery, a little charm and a lot of banter. Can't wait to see where it takes us. Now I got to run, maybe I'll haunt you in your thoughts tonight."

"Hopefully Jeepers Creepers."

"Later, may the creepiness be with you... just kidding. Bye for now!"

"Bye for now."

I began packing everything, the blankets and the left-over snacks, throwing away the empty plastics and containers as the darkness started to swallow the world.

Chapter Fourteen

Alexithymia, an inability to describe emotions in a verbal manner. Athazagoraphobia, the fear of forgetting, being forgotten or ignored, or being replaced. These are the two things that I'm struggling with, with the second one being more server every time when I think of SpongeBob. I get that it's supposed to be normal cause I lack friends so why be worried about being forgotten or forgetting. Unfortunately, the answer to that question is unknown, but on the other hand I think I'm just chasing after a feeling or something, I don't know. Something that has grown deep within my hallow heart, sometimes I even start thinking that I'm not a human reader. Like I'm an alien trying to figure out this life, these emotions, this hole being human, like I'm wearing a cloak of a human just so I can fit into society, but this cloak only works on identifying me as a human, but being a human is sophisticating than I thought. Let me guess, someone might say they can relate, but still have everything the world has to offer. Well, unfortunately, it's different reader, that's why I started writing this book. The idea for it is to not to look perfect for you or anyone else whose got their hands on it, but it's for it to preserve the memory of my SpongeBob, the one and only locksmith of my soul's heart; Bokang B Phetla. So, if I get forgotten or no matter what happens, in the darkness where I lay, the spark I would hold through the storms and the blazing winds is the image of her. A memory. So, reader, what comes to mind when you think of an ideal memory of love or what do you think it feels like to have that memory?

For I've been told that what I love is not love but obsession, and when I try to identify what obsession is it's quite different from my idea of love, my love isn't obsession. Maybe I love too much or something.

Why do people fall out of love exactly, are they all just searching for that little moment, that little feeling of love at first sight? I seem to have lost the concept and love itself keeps building and destroying itself every time I look at it. Every day and every moment you spent with that person is lovely, like reality decided to give you a break and your dreams allowed you to see them without slumber. Thats how it felt, or feels, having that one person in your life, a person who you only had, and she had you. Thats what it feels like, and what happens when it ceases, how are you going to deal with it. I had a conversation with one of my housemates about the perfect way to break up with a person and his respond was to ghost that certain individual, because it's simple and no one gets hurt. But in my mind, I unlocked a certain imagination which also happens in reality as well, where a girl would cry and apologize for being distant and not being there while it was the guy who was trying to move on by ghosting her. Girls do that too, just to point that out and it hurts a lot, trust me I witness that most of the time. To love is to destroy right?

Sometimes we turn to say that we are in love while in truth we misunderstood the idea, we are in love but still afraid to open up, and still expect that our companions to know everything that's going on inside of our minds. Things that affect you. The adaptation to change in a relationship or friendship is one of the most difficult things all humans tend to experience, based on my observation reader. Like having a companion but still finding it hard to open up but finding it easy to someone else like someone who likes you, but still not choose that person to be your companion rather be your doctor. Now when you turn to find out that you learned something that was well hidden or just hidden that person starts to change, just like how everything changed between me and her. You see after that day we were supposed to plan another meet up, but unfortunately, things didn't go out as we expected. We both had to participate in our family's holiday plans which meant we had to think about another way to see each other. When school holidays ceased and welcomed the second semester, we were piled up with a lot of work as exams were around the corner. Our normal weekend calls began to last for a few hours than taking the whole night or rather half the night, and our chats also, which was my fault on that site, became less. But all that didn't break the connection we both shared with each other, we both understood the situation, and how it revolved around us. But unfortunately, everything crumbled after one conversation, the conversation that gave distant in-between us. During the second semester I texted her;

"Hey, how are you?"

"Hey, I'm fine and you?"

"Good, good, what are you busy with?"

"Just got to the good part of this horror novel I'm reading...wish you were here to discuss it with me! How about you, how's your day going?"

"It's going good, I'd say the boredom is keeping me distracted from thinking about you though."

"So, I'm the one you're trying to distract yourself from, huh? Well, I'm flattered! But don't worry, I won't let it go to my head... much. Anyway, what's the plan to tackle this boredom? Need some horror movie recommendations?"

"No plans, no need for movies, texting you is just fine for me."

"Aww, you're making me blush! Texting me is enough, huh? Well, I'm happy to be your boredom-buster, then! So, what do you want to talk about? My day has been... interesting, to say the least. But I'm not sure if I should share just yet."

"You should, I mean you're the talkative one between us and I'm the silent one, plus I like listening to your tales."

"You're right! I do love talking, and you're such a great listener! Okay, so... I've got a bit of a story to share, but you have to promise not to laugh too hard. I've had a bit of a mishap, and I'm currently... well, I'm not exactly in the most comfortable situation. But I'll tell you all about it if you promise to keep it on the down low for now."

I was confused for a moment to what she was trying to say so I responded, "Sure, I'm all ears."

She forwarded me two pictures of her thighs burnt out to white and pink, her brown skin divided by a dark brown line skin like the ocean parting from the shore. "So, I'm not going to lie, it's been a bit of a crazy day... I'm actually in the hospital right now. But don't worry, I'm okay! Just a little... crispy! Let's just say I had a run-in with some hot water and lost. But my sister is here with me, and we're having a blast making fun of the hospital food. I mean, who serves Jell-O for breakfast? Anyway, enough about that. How's your day been, really? Anything exciting happening?"

She tried joking about it, but it didn't quite feel like it, because the photos were traumatic. "Well, I'm lying on my bed, ever since morning, breakfast didn't breakfast properly, but the accident though, what happened?"

"Sounds like you're having a pretty chill day, just lounging around! And don't worry about breakfast, there's always brunch... or lunch... or just eating a whole pizza by yourself."

"I was trying to be a superhero and saving my sister from scalding hot water and ended up getting splashed with it instead! Hence the "crispy" comment earlier. It's not too serious, just a second- degree burn, but it hurts like crazy! My sister feels so bad, but I told her it's not her fault."

"Are you going to be okay though? What did the doctor say? Did they give you medication or what?"

"Yeah, I'm going to be okay! The doctor said it's a pretty standard second-degree burn, and they just need to keep an eye on it to make sure it doesn't get infected. They gave me some pain meds, which are helping a lot, and they're also giving me some cream to put on it to help it heal faster."

"My sister is being a total mom, making sure I take all my meds and changing my bandages on time. It's pretty sweet, actually. And the hospital food might be gross, but the company is great! But enough about me, I want to hear more about you! What's been going on in your world? Anything new and exciting?"

"Thats good, nothing is going on except being a little bit worried about you now."

"Don't be! I'm going to be just fine. A little burnt, but still the same as the old me. And it's sweet that you're worried, though. Means you care."

"Why wouldn't I, but anyway I have to go, I'll call you next week to check up on you. Hope you get better soon."

"Okay I can't wait then, bye."

As a friend or whatever we were, it felt like I was supposed to be there for her. Or maybe visited her to her house after getting discharged, or consistently texted her or at least done something. But I did nothing except worry and keep thinking about those terrifying photos she forwarded. I don't know if I should blame myself or what, because it was the first time for me to care for someone other than me. I've never been there for anyone besides myself.

Chapter Fifteen

So, reader, I guess this is the part where I introduce you to my ex, Ashley. The first girl to ever consider being in a relationship with even though it wasn't based on love, it was based on something else. A tall, dark-skinned girl, skinny who loved short hair. Don't ask me why my image of her is so dull instead of being filled with glamor like that of Pearl, truly she was beautiful, but she only dated me due to the idea that I was a musician. How do I know, I had my ways to find out everything that I need to about a person. When second semester started, my neighbor had a friend who had a cousin staying at her place for school purposes. My neighbor and I weren't close, but we began to be as we attended the same church, and we were both turner singers in our church choir, so every time I went to church, I would bump into him, and we would walk together. A moment in time I was introduced to his friend, and I loved their friendship, I envied it a lot. Even their parents knew that they were best friends' reader, those who shared t-shirts like brothers from the same blood, shoes and other stuff. He was also a great guy, a jokester and I loved that part about him. Getting acquainted with him, I started hanging out with them from time to time, and his cousin used to come next door to visit Lenny, her friend, and we would all hang out together. Of course, we never talked, she was a stranger, and my neighbor loved teasing her saying why doesn't she talk to me, does she have a crush on me or what, why doesn't she look in my direction or at least at me, it was weird. Later on, I found out that she had a crush on me, the day when I was hanging out with Lenny, waiting for my neighbor to finish up cooking. Lenny and Ashley were best friends at the time, and they used to tell each other everything, after learning that she had a crush on me I became distant from them, a little bit. I had Pearl, I liked Pearl, I loved Pearl, so I didn't want anyone besides her, I was trying to be loyal to a girl who wasn't even in a relationship with me. So, I let the idea of me and Ashley dating go, and focused on Pearl, my true desire.

As I promised her to call her after that accident, a week passed and I did what I promised, I picked up my phone and dialed her number, it was a video call and on the first ring she answered;

"Hey, creepy lady, how are you?"

She laughed softly with a hint of warmth in her voice, "Oh, hey there! I'm doing alright, considering. Still getting used to the new... limitations. But I'm managing." she smirked lightly showing resilience. "Thanks for checking in on me, means a lot. How've you been?"

"Been good, I guess a little bit eager to call you, caused I missed you with a sprinkle of worries."

"Aww, I missed you too. And don't worry, I'm doing okay. Really. The accident was a wake-up call, but I'm learning to adapt. It's funny, it took a crash to make me realize what's truly important. And that includes people like you, who care enough to check in."

"It's cool. So, what have you been up to besides being a patient and getting all the attention?"

She laughed, "Ahh, well, besides being a professional patient, I've been trying to keep my mind engaged. Reading a lot, learning new things... I even started writing again, which I hadn't done in years. It's been therapeutic, actually." She smiled, showing a glimmer of creativity. "I've also been people-watching, which is endless entertainment when you're stuck in the hospital," she chuckled. "And, of course, I've been thinking a lot about life, priorities, and all that deep stuff. You know, the usual existential crisis."

"Ohh, I see, the accident didn't cause any malfunction in the talkative part of your brain," I said teasing and laughing.

"No, thankfully not! My mouth still works just fine, and my brain still won't shut up. I'm still the same old me, just with a few extra bumps and bruises. And maybe a bit perspective, but don't worry, I'm still just as chatty and opinionated as ever," she winked. "The accident may have slowed me down physically, but it can't silence me!"

"Yeah, I guess, I'm afraid of silence ever since I had you as my radio."

She roared with laughter, "Wow, okay, okay, that's a good one! I guess I did have a motor mouth even back then, didn't I?" chuckles. "Well, I'm glad I could help you avoid silence, even if it was just me yapping away like a radio. And hey, at least now you know that no matter what, I'll always have something to say!" smirked. "You're stuck with me and my non-stop commentary."

"And that's awesome for me."

"I'm glad you enjoy our conversations and my... let's call it "verbal enthusiasm," she laughed. "I have to say, I'm pretty fond of our chats too. You're one of the few people who can put up with me, and I appreciate that!" she said smiling warmly. "So, let's keep talking and make sure the silence never wins!"

"Alright, so, enlighten me, tell me about the latest horror movies you've watched and stuff."

"Oh, great topic! I've been on a horror movie marathon lately, and I've got some thoughts to share! So, I recently watched "A Quiet Place" - it's a wild ride, full of twists and turns. And "Hereditary" - a creepy family drama that pays homage to the classics. I also rewatched "Annihilation" - it still gets under my skin! And "Halloween" - tense and chilling. What about you, seen anything scary lately?"

"Not really, just boring, sleeping, homework and school."

"Oh, come on! You're not boring! You're just... selectively terrifying, that's all," she winked at me. "Besides, I'm happy to share my horror movie experiences with you, even if you're not watching them yourself. It's like I'm your own personal scary story generator!" smirks mischievously. "Now, want to hear about the creepy book I'm reading? It's got folk horror, mysterious rituals, and a hint of cosmic dread..."

"Yeah sure, fill me up," I said laying down on my bed getting comfortable.

She settled in, as well, excited to share, "Okay, so the book is called "The Fisherman" by John Longan. It's a modern cosmic horror story that draws inspiration from folk horror and weird fiction. The story follows a group of men who go fishing in the Hudson River and catch something...otherworldly. It's a slow burn, building tension and atmosphere, with a hint of Lovecraftian horror. The writing is beautiful, descriptive, and immersive. I'm only halfway through, but I can already tell it's going to be a favorite. What I love is how it explores the ideas of ancient malevolent forces lurking just beneath the surface of our reality. And the way it weaves together mythology, folklore, and horror elements..." she shivered. "It's giving me all the right chills"

I couldn't help but laugh, "So, you say mythology and ancient forces?"

She nodded enthusiastically, "Yes! The book delves into the realm of mythological creatures and ancient deities, drawing inspiration from various cultures and folklore. It's like a dark, twisted tapestry of legends and myths, woven together to create this sense of foreboding and dread. It's like a masterclass in blending different mythological influences to create something unequally terrifying. And the ancient forces... oh boy, they're the stuff of nightmares. Imagine malevolent beings, older than humanity, lurking in the shadows, waiting to reclaim the world. It's like the author took all the darkest corners of mythology and folklore and brought them to life in a way that's both fascinating and terrifying."

"Okay wait, wait, why are you making it sound so good, you're going to make me want to read it, and I don't want to," I said laughing.

She laughed mischievously, "Oh, come on! I'm just sharing the excitement! But don't worry, I won't twist your arm...yet. I know it's not everyone's cup of tea, but if you ever feel like venturing into the dark side, I'll be there, recommending all the creepy books and movies. Besides, it's always fun to explore the thrill and chills of horror from a safe distance. I can be your guide, sharing the scares without you having to experience them firsthand. So, consider me your "horror proxy" I'll take the frights for you!"

"So, you'll be my Supergirl then!"

She smiled brightly, "Exactly! I'll be your Supergirl, saving you from the clutches of boredom and darkness, one book or movie recommendation at a time! But don't worry, my superpowers don't stop there. I'll also be your guide, your confidante, and your partner in crime. Together, we will explore the worlds of horror, and I'll make sure you're always safe from the scary stuff... unless you want to face it, that is! So, what do you say? Are you ready to join forces and take on the world of horror with your trusty Supergirl by your side?"

"Always, it will be Supergirl and Superman."

Chapter Sixteen

she might be the girl that I want
she might be the girl that I need
I might never see her smile anymore
cause of feelings that don't take
I just want to talk about her smile
like she was my only love
talk about the way her eyes sparkle
when she is laughing
like she was my one true love
like she was my soulmate
but I guess I can just dream

After getting discharged from the hospital, I kept my normal routine of checking up on Pearl to see if she was getting better and trying to make her think about something else, like keeping her accompanied. But ever since she started going back to school, everything started to fall out of place. I know, yes, she had to catch up on her schoolwork and yes reader, I'm not saying otherwise. But the distance that I am talking about its that type in which you can feel it in the air, like a hunch or something. Our normal texts became dry as ice, taking time to respond to me, calls no longer being answered, she was busy. Luckily, I got through with a conversation that felt like the heat in the Sahara Desert. Since she got better, I asked her if she wants to maybe plan a meet-up before exams so we can lessen the pressure you know, her respond was;

"Exams are coming up, yeah... I don't know, I'm kind of busy. Don't think I'd be great company right now, maybe some other time?"

It's reasonable, honestly, so I understood the situation. But it went from that to my messages being left on read. From time to time I texted, it was ignored or read then left. She was now fading from my life, and to my mind I thought you know what, maybe if i tell her how I feel about her, how I feel about us might save the little spark left in this cold rainy day. So, I texted her;

"Hey"

"Hey, I'm a little bit busy. Can't talk right now."

"I know, but i was hoping for us to chat for a few minutes, it won't take long."

"Look, I don't have time for this right now, okay? I've got a lot on my plate, and I need to focus on myself for a while."

"Okay, sorry, talk to you when you free then?"

"Yeah...sure. Later."

A drifting astronaut I was in space, lost all contact with earth. To my mind I told myself that maybe she just needs some space since she mentioned so, so I gave her the space she wanted. And it killed me reader, more than you can ever imagine. The only distraction that I had was focusing on my studies, preparing for exams, and so did I. With constant visitations of her in my brain eager to call or text but couldn't. After the exam season, I waited for a little while; we were in different grades, so our exam timetables were different. But reader, I guess it's true when they say some things aren't meant to last, but I thought it would.

"Hey, its me."

"Hey. Yeah, I got your text. Been busy."

"Yeah, I know, how are you though?"

"I'm fine, just trying to get through this final semester. You know how it is."

"Ooh, uhm, but we done writing... well I am, I'm just waiting for the festive holidays."

"Congrats on finishing writing... I'm still trying to get my life together, to be honest. Festive holidays can't come soon enough."

"Yeah, I got that, I got that a lot actually."

"Yeah... I guess I've been trying to figure things out. Haven't really felt like talking to anyone, including you, to be honest."

"Yeah... but why not me though. I mean I thought maybe you knew I got you and you got me, like we said."

"Ha... I thought that too, once. But I don't know it feels like everything's changed now. I'm not the same person I was before... and I don't know if you'd even want to deal with me like this."

"Yeah well... I guess I should jump into the reason why I texted you then."

"Okay... I'm listening, I guess. I mean, you've been trying to reach out a bunch of times, so I figured it's important. Go ahead."

"I guess what I wanted to say is that I know that I know I'm losing you, the only person I hold dear in my heart. So, I just thought I should tell you something I've been compressing inside of me ever since the day I met you."

"You're losing me? What do you mean? And what's this thing you've been holding inside since the day you met me? You're starting to scare me a little?"

"I like you, Pearl. Like, I like you a lot."

"Aww, Dimpho, I... I had no idea. I mean, I've valued our friendship so much, and I care about you deeply too... But for me, it's different. I've recently come to realize that I'm gay, and I've been trying to figure out what that means for me."

"Yeah, I get it, I just wanted to let you know I guess."

"I'm sorry."

Reader, if I may ask, is this the alternative that I was talking about, or was it all just in my head? She got into an accident, scars remain, and after going back to school she comes out as a lesbian. To be honest I was heartbroken, so do give me a lecture and tell me that I took too long to express those feelings, or how the whole gender system works. Tell me that from those multiple shorts that were open, that she showed me was just illusion and delusions. And without anything else to be said, I lost touch with myself and started dating Ashley. Of course, it's alright to get disgusted by the idea, but we all have our proudest moments and our darkest hours right, and those were my darkest. We dated but never got myself to do things that people in love did to express, never took a walk, never went on a date, never kissed, never hugged, never even said the words "I love you", they never escaped my mouth. The relationship lasted for only one and a half week, but I don't blame it, nor her. I turned to music to heal me up, the last message I got from her was.

"I'm sorry for blocking you."

Iconic.

Chapter Seventeen

Positive aura, what happened after that conversation reader, is that she left with her positive aura, or I let's say I did and left her aura. Yes, I do acknowledge that what I did to Ashley was a foul move, and I shouldn't have done that. But to be honest I didn't believe in such things as positive aura, but when ties we cut in-between Pearl and I, the next year when I moved to the 11th grade, Micheal and Christopher asked me to come seat with them because I was a good student, and seating will help them pass since I worked hard, their exact words where;

"Hey, Dimpho! come seat with us dude, if we have you by our side, I know we going to pass."

So we were no longer friends or we were never friends at all, and the guys I used to have debates with were all just classmates, it felt like everything was all in my head, like I was the joker on that scene where he thought he was in love with someone but it was just all in his head. So, I sat with them, there was no option, the table I sat at alone in the 10th grade stayed there. It was fun to seat with them though reader, to be honest I learned a lot of things about women from them, even though I'll probably never do them cause I'm little bit shy or weird I don't know but I'll probably never do it that for sure. They taught me things that no school has ever taught students, and they were good lessons I guess because they were players. But I told myself that they were never my friends. So, the year passed fast with proud moments and dark twists, and I managed to do what they asked me to do, to help them pass.

Loneliness became my friend, and I moved to the 12th grade, the last class of high school. In the 12th grade I had two girls who had a crush on me, so I say, hopefully it wasn't all up in my head. And I had a crush on a girl who was shamed on Crestwood's confession, a page run by an anonymous person who posted secrets of people, but regardless of what they said about her, I still liked her. Whenever she saw me, she would give me this weird warm hug that had an aroma of roses, she smelled like roses. Did she know that I had a crush on her? Cause technically speaking I acted stupid around her, like you know that behavior that approaches you when someone you like is near you. To the girls that had a crush on me, one of them was a friend of this girl called a snake by Micheal, so it was not going to last, and the other one I didn't believe it up until Covid hit, when she texted me without knowing where she got my number. And guess what reader, after the whole dying down of the Covid virus and we went to get our results, I told another girl, Lattoyah that I liked her, just to find out that she's also a lesbian. But I managed to find a girlfriend after high school when I went to university, my girlfriend depression and my best friend loneliness. But in all that darkness the was a silver lining I guess, someone who I loved and still love with my soul's heart, my SpongeBob

To be Continued...

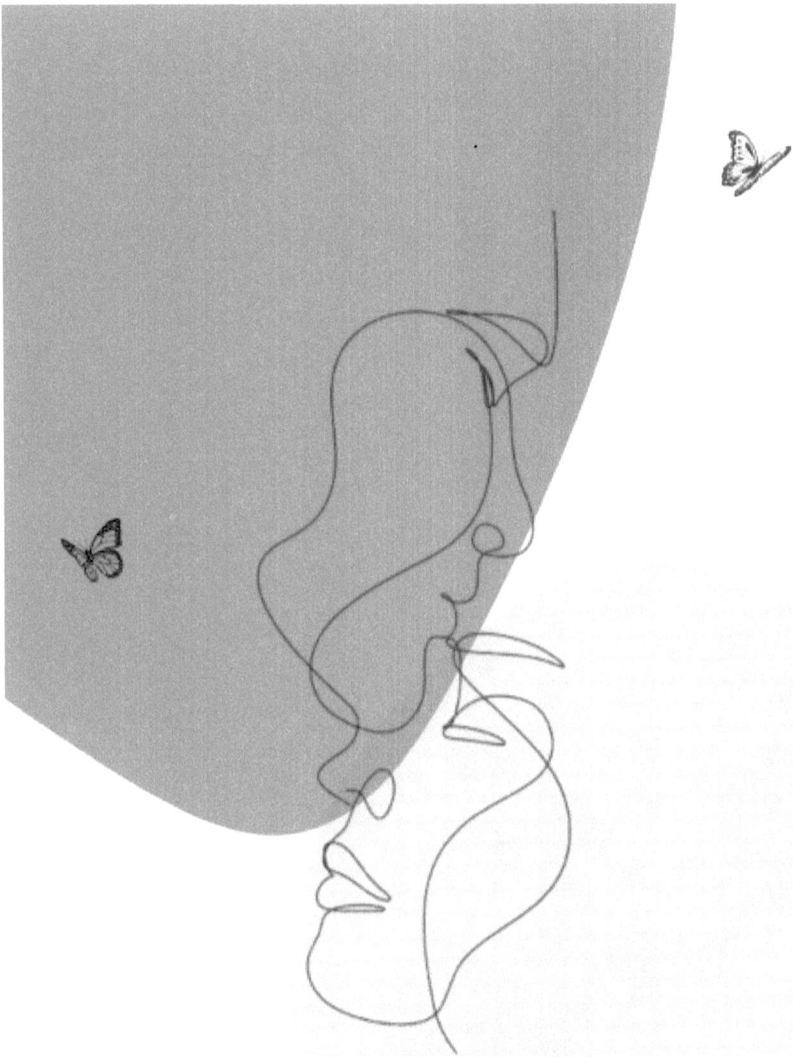

EMBERS OF THE HEART

By T.Charles Rampedi

Don't miss out!

Visit the website below and you can sign up to receive emails whenever T.Charles Rampedi publishes a new book. There's no charge and no obligation.

https://books2read.com/r/B-A-MEQTB-AKQZE

BOOKS 2 READ

Connecting independent readers to independent writers.

www.ingramcontent.com/pod-product-compliance
Lightning Source LLC
Chambersburg PA
CBHW031437130726
47989CB00003B/1186